AF395936

The Synoptic
Book of Esther

Register as a Friend of EnvelopeBooks

We invite the first owner of this copy of The Synoptic Book of Esther to record their name with the publisher.

By registering yourself as the book's original owner, you become a Friend of EnvelopeBooks and a part of the EnvelopeBooks family. Registration shows that you love books, as we do, and allows us to tell you what other publications we think you might like.

Fill in your name and the date in the space below, then take a photo of your inscription and send it to us via www.envelopebooks.co.uk.

We very much look forward to welcoming you.

By order,
The Publisher

Your name ....

Date of Purchase ....

The Synoptic Book of Esther

With an introduction,
endnotes, and the
Septuagint text in an appendix

Edited and Introduced by Stephen Games PhD

44

EnvelopeBooks

ENVELOPEBOOKS
First edition 2015 (paperback): *The Reader's Megillah*
Second edition 2016 (paperback):
Revisions: March 2016
Third edition 2026 (hardback): *The Synoptic Book of Esther*

Published 2026 in the UK and USA by EnvelopeBooks

12 Wellfield Avenue, London N10 2EA, England
116 West 73rd Street, New York, NY 10023

www.envelopebooks.co.uk

Cover design by Stephen Games | Booklaunch

Main text set in Minion Pro Regular 10.5/12.6 and Adobe Hebrew 15/18-19.
Typeset by New Premises

A CIP catalogue record for this title is available from the British Library and the Library of Congress Cataloging-in-Publication Data

EnvelopeBooks 44
ISBN 9781915023759

Contents

Foreword   i

Introduction   1

The Synoptic Megilla in English and Hebrew   21

Endnotes   52

Appendix: The Septuagint Megillah in English   62

Illustrations by Gustave Doré

Queen Vashti refuses to obey the command of King Ahasuerus   21

Mordecai is led on horseback through Shushan by Haman   38

Queen Esther faints at the prospect of having to beg the king to protect the Jews without her being sure of his favour (according to Septuagint Addition D)   39

Queen Esther accuses Haman   50

The enemies of the Jews are defeated in Shushan   51

Foreword

British polymath Stephen Games (art, design, architecture, literature, biography) has focused his perceptive attention on the short but fascinating Book of Esther—the *Megillah*.

He takes a tradition–sympathetic perspective, discussing the critical and Persian-Greek historical context, but ultimately coming down to a very interesting hypothesis. Examining the text in great detail (the book is worth it to follow the endnotes alone), he discerns two strands in the composition: one 'brief and unornamented', the second 'more detailed and florid'. He suggests—really only suggests—that the first voice is that of Mordecai, and the second that of Esther. The book, he believes, has dual authorship.

To demonstrate this, both the Hebrew and the English texts are laid out on the page in accordance with his theory.

I learned a great deal from this—from the Introduction, from the analysis and from the copious notes to the text. Despite the fact that the *Megillah* is one of the most closely followed publicly read texts, the festive context means it is easy to miss a great deal of (often contradictory) detail.

Dr Games's unusual publication may not be the easiest text to take to synagogue on the festival of Purim (because of the text layout) but my heretical suggestion is that this slim and unobtrusive volume is an ideal choice to slip into a *tallit* bag, to read during sermons on the Sabbaths preceding the festival . . . and maybe afterwards.

Worth noting, too, the clarity and quality of the writing, and the appeal of the translation.

Recommended, challenging and enjoyable.

Paul Shaviv
New York
2016

Introduction

The Book of Esther is an imperfect biblical text. In this it is not unique. All biblical texts are imperfect, as anyone would expect of documents that have survived long periods of time. Language changes, laws change, cultural attitudes change. It should come as no surprise to find that texts change too, even when one of the reasons for first writing them down, rather than committing them to memory, was, presumably, to guarantee their integrity.

For literalists, acknowledging textual imperfection in religious works has been problematic, especially in relation to the Five Books of Moses—the *Chumash*—in which is embodied the *Torah* (the Jewish Law). The Five Books are honoured by traditionalists as the word of God and thus as necessarily perfect. The Book of Esther—*Megillat Esther*—is not, however, a sacred text in the same sense. It was a late addition to the Jewish biblical canon, and was supposedly admitted only because it was ancient and written in Hebrew, told a story of Jewish survival, reinforced Jewish national identity, and provided the only available scriptural evidence for the Jewish festival of Purim, albeit without mentioning God.

According to religious scholarship, the book is set in the time of Xerxes I, with whom the king in the story, Ahasuerus, is usually identified, and its writing is traditionally credited to one or both of its two Jewish characters: Esther, its eponymous heroine, and Mordecai, her cousin and adoptive father, though neither appears in the first person.

The identity of both characters gives rise to immediate questions. The text first introduces Esther by another name—Hadassah—for reasons that are not explained, and, depending on how one reads it, offers three different reasons for her being adopted: that she was the daughter of Mordecai's uncle, that she had no parents, and that she was good-looking. It only identifies her real father when referring to him in a later passage.

Greater difficulties than this come thick and fast. The text says of Mordecai that he was 'the son of Jair, the son of Shimei, the son of Kish' and 'a Benjamite, who had been carried away from Jerusalem with the captives that had been carried away with Jeconiah, king of Judah, whom Nebuchadnezzar the king of Babylon had carried away'. This cannot be taken at face value because King Jeconiah was among the first to be removed to Babylon following Nebuchadnezzar's conquest of Jerusalem in 597 BCE, and that would have made Mordecai implausibly old at the time of the story.

There was a second deportation ten years later, in 587, and a third in 582, but the account is clear that Mordecai was one of the captives carried away with the king rather than subsequently. Jews were allowed to return to Judea in 539, when the Babylonian Empire fell to the Achaemenid Persians, but many chose to stay and live under Persian rule (in what we would now call the Neo-Babylonian Empire) and Mordecai would seem to have been one of them.

Babylon's conqueror was Cyrus the Great, and Cyrus was succeeded by his son Cambyses II, who was succeeded in turn by Darius I. Among Darius's many wives was Atossa, a sister of Cambyses, who bore him four sons, one of whom was Xerxes I, Cyrus's grandson, who reigned after Darius's death in 486 BCE. The events in the Book of Esther start in the third year of Ahasuerus's reign; Esther would have become a member of the royal household in about the seventh year; and Haman's plot against the Jews—the subject of the book—would have begun in the twelfth year and been finally foiled in the thirteenth.

If Ahasuerus had been Xerxes, these events would have taken place around 473 BCE. According to this reckoning, Mordecai would have been born in pre-exilic Jerusalem and would have lived through the entirety of the Babylonian captivity and the reigns of two Persian kings before going on to enjoy a productive life as second-in-command to a third, all of which would put him well into his second century when the events in Shushan take place. Had Esther been the daughter of his uncle, she would have been over a hundred as well, rather than *'naara y'fat to'ar v'tovat mar'eh'* (a maiden of beautiful form and good to look at).

Mordecai's chronology is more plausible if Ahasuerus was not Xerxes but Cyrus, the first Persian king after the Babylonians, but he would still have to have been brought to Babylon as a baby for him to have been at least sixty years old when the Esther story starts. There is a choice, therefore, between accepting the interior account of Mordecai's life, which makes the externals impossible, and accepting the exterior historicity of Ahasuerus which makes the internals impossible.

An alternative reading is that 'who had been carried away from Jerusalem' refers not to Mordecai but to the last-named in the list of captives: Kish, his great-grandfather. This interpretation helps get round the timeline problem. If a generation is reckoned as roughly twenty-five years, Mordecai could have been born at any time during the Babylonian capitivity, in which case the timings and text can be reconciled. Treating Kish rather than Mordecai as the captive is not, however, the most natural reading, nor was it the traditional reading until required by the needs of modern literary scholarship and archaeology.

Another problem is that 'Kish' is a Babylonian name—indeed, it is the name of a town about fifteen miles from the city of Babylon—and it is unlikely that a pre-exilic Jew would have been given a Babylonian name.

According to the Book of Esther, Mordecai lived not in Babylon but in Shushan. Shushan is usually identified with Susa, the ancient Sumerian town where the prophets Daniel and Nehemiah had lived during the Babylonian exile and that dated back to the fifth century BCE. Susa, 300 kilometres to the east of the city of Babylon and lying between the Dez and Karkheh rivers,[1] became the capital of a small but powerful province called Shushan or Ŝuŝan; late in the third millennium BCE it was taken over by Elamites— in biblical terms the descendants of Elam, the eldest son of Noah's son Shem.

Shushan grew to be economically, politically and culturally important before being sacked by Ashurbanipal in 646 BCE. It then struggled on as a fragmented province until captured between 540 and 539 by Cyrus who, in recognition of its long and important history, adopted the honorific 'King of Shushan and Anshan' as one of his many titles.

Cyrus died in 530. Eight years later, Darius—a distant cousin and not an heir—seized the throne, and Susa/Shushan enjoyed an astonishing revival. An extensive programme of civic works was started on, with Darius building a new fortress as his winter residence, promoting the Elamite language as the principal language of the Persian Achaemenid empire and sustaining Elamite deities, cults and priests. The town also became the setting for the earliest surviving play of Aeschylus, *The Persians*, written in 472—the same year in which Haman is said to have hatched his plans for the Jews, if Ahasuerus and Xerxes are cognate. The Esther story can even be linked to Susa's Persian renaissance and, in this context, the description at the start of the book of the luxury of Ahasuerus's palace and lifestyle is not insignificant.

Efforts have been made to identify Mordecai. The name is not Jewish but Aramaic and derives from Marduk,[2] a Mesopotamian god for whom Nebuchadnezzar rebuilt the grand Ésagila temple next to the Etemenanki ziggurat (the inspiration for the Tower of Babel/Babylon). Aramaic ritual texts unearthed between 1936 and 1938 from Persepolis,[3] which was Darius's other main centre of reconstruction, include 'Marduka' or 'Marduku' among the names of court officials, and this appears to concur with the high status that *Megillat*

---

1 The Karkheh is said to be another name for Gihon, one of the four rivers serving the Garden of Eden.
2 Egyptian Amun; Greek Zeus.
3 Bowman, R.A., *Aramaic Ritual Texts from Persepolis, Oriental Institute Publications 91*, Chicago: The University of Chicago Press, 1970.

Esther's closing verses ascribe to Mordecai. Although at first sight anomalous, the naming of Mordecai after Babylon's principal deity alerts us only to the pervasiveness of Babylonian culture, to which its Jews were no more immune than any other group within the Babylonian sphere of influence.

It is also possible that the word 'Marduk' was adopted by Jews in Babylon as a local word for deity, just as English-speaking Jews commonly say 'God' rather than 'Eil' or 'Elohim'. We can suspect this because there is so much other evidence for the transformative effect of Babylon on Jewish experience. Over the course of nearly sixty years, Judaism—hitherto a variant Canaanite culture—became an Akkadian culture, losing its Paleo-Hebrew writing in favour of the Aramaic script that it still uses, and adopting Babylonian names for the months.[4] Jewish culture became impregnated with numerous harmless pagan references. Tammuz, the adopted name for the fourth month, for example, was taken from an ancient Akkadian nature god, which no doubt had no more significance than the fact that four of the names of English weekdays derive from Norse gods (Tyr, Odin, Thor and Frigge). That 'Mordecai' may have meant 'a follower or servant of God' or 'Marduk lives' (*Marduk chai*) also did not make it contentious or heretical. By the same token, it is likely that the name 'Esther' is a variant of 'Ishtar', the Babylonian fertility goddess.

The fact that Mordecai and Esther had Babylonian names alerts us also to the likelihood that both were born in Babylon as the children or grandchildren or great-grandchildren of the Jerusalem captives, rather than their having been taken into captivity themselves. In the case of Mordecai in particular, this calls into question the traditional reading.

The *Megillah* text answers numerous questions concerning the events in the Esther story. We learn for example that, as a result of their exile from Jerusalem, Jews had dispersed all over the region, to the extent that by the time of Haman's plot, they could be found '*b'chol m'dinot*' ('in all the provinces') of the king. That is to say, they were recent immigrants (albeit originally unwilling immigrants) to what had been Babylonia but, as we know from the refusal of many to return to Judea, must have adapted well to their new conditions.

We can also suppose that unless Haman's plot really was triggered only by what Haman took as Mordecai's discourtesy, the Jews' presence was widely resented. This can be inferred because Mordecai tells Esther not to disclose her Jewish identity to the king before the clash with Haman takes place, and also because Ahasuerus seems at first untroubled by Haman's proposal for the Jews' wholesale slaughter. To be Jewish in the time of Ahasuerus was evidently a handicap.

So far so clear. The story of a plot against the Jews and of the reprisals that ended it can be anchored to a tenable timeline. Admittedly, we no longer have any external corroboration for it: *The Book of the Chronicles of the Kings of Media and Persia*, otherwise known as *The Chronicles of King Ahasuerus*, reference to which can be found in *Esther* 2:23, 6:1 and 10:2, and in *Nehemiah* 12:23, has not survived. In spite of that, the coherence of the narrative makes at least a small claim on historicity.

At the same time, even if the Esther story were true and authored by Mordecai, or by Mordecai and Esther, rather than by other later hands and rather than being a narrative invention, it has textual imperfections: certain passages break the rules of even the most basic storytelling, and the fact that the entire text has remained unchanged for millennia suggests that these imperfections were intrinsic to its history and fundamental to its writing.

In Chapter One, for example, the king's feast is first referred to as lasting 180 days and then as lasting seven days. The reader is asked by traditional commmntators to understand from this that the king gave a second, shorter feast after the first one. Ostensibly this is credible, except that the character of the writing belies such an interpretation. Although magnificent, the first feast is described very briefly (1:3–4), in the manner of an official record. This brevity leaves ambiguities about whom the feast was aimed at, prompting the later addition of three explanatory passages. These inform us that the feast was meant

---

4   Before the exile, only four Hebrew months had names: two in the spring (Aviv and Ziv) and two in the autumn (Eithanim and Bul). These became respectively Nissan, Iyar, Tishri and Cheshvan. The remaining eight months had previously been known only by their numerical place in the calendar. Thus the fourth month became Tammuz, and the fifth month became Av, meaning fiery or hot. It is significant, therefore, that when the Book of Esther says 'In the first month, which is the month Nissan,' or 'in the tenth month, which is the month Teveth,' it is not being pedantic or repetitive but identfying the month in the Hebrew, then the Babylonian, custom.

for 'all [the king's] princes and his servants', 'the army of Persia and Media' and 'the nobles and princes of the provinces'. Albeit sequential, these passages cannot be inclusive because of the duplication of 'nobles and princes': they must therefore be variants. The second account (1:5–8) is quite different: it is literary, atmospheric and detailed, and because of the difference in tone, it is best read not as an amplification of the earlier feast or even as an addition to it but as separate, alternative and contradictory.

Conflicting accounts of Ahasuerus's feast in Chapter One of the *Megillah* have no significant bearing on the story. Nor do those at the start of Chapter Eight, where the queen's plea that Ahasuerus annul Haman's decree is introduced in two different ways. In the first (8:3), where we are given only a summary of her actions without hearing the words she speaks, Esther falls at the king's feet and, weeping, begs him *'l'haavir et-roat'*—to 'put away the mischief' that Haman had 'devised against the Jews'. In the longer, second version (8:4–6), we get details, a spoken request, a reminder of what Haman had wanted to do, and a pathetic apostrophe: 'How can I endure to see the evil that shall come unto my people? or how can I endure to see the destruction of my kindred?'

We also get in this second version two very similar phrases with variant wording: in addressing the king, Esther says (8:5) 'If it please the king and if I have found favour in his sight' and '[if] the thing seem right before the king and I be pleasing in his eyes'; and in the following line (8:6) 'for how can I endure to see the evil that shall come unto my people?' and 'how can I endure to see the destruction of my kindred?' In both cases, the alternative phrase is a near duplication of the phrase it precedes (and in the standard English translation of the Hebrew, the alternative statement in 8:6 is introduced with 'or').

The pairing of similar statements is a familiar formula in Hebrew lyric poetry: the Psalms—the model for all subsequent lyric prayers—are characterised almost throughout by their antiphonal structure:

> Happy is the man who did not walk in the counsel of the wicked, nor stand in the way of sinners …
> (Psalms 1:1)

The duplications embedded in Esther's pleas

conform to this convention. They are poetic and refer not to pluralities but variants. The rest of *Esther* is anything but poetic, but still conforms to this structural model. We have a literary precedent, therefore, for reading its repetitions as singularities, as will be shown.

The two examples quoted above—in chapters One and Eight—have little impact on the narrative. Other imperfections are more difficult. One appears in Chapter Five. Here again there are two accounts: the first briefer, the second more expansive and atmospheric. In the first, we learn in just two lines (5:4–5) that after the king asks Esther what she wants, she begs him and Haman to attend her banquet *'hayom'* (today). She clearly wants a favour but seeks to ask it under more auspicious conditions. The king registers this and replies, simply, *'maharu et-Haman laasot et-d'var Esther'* (Make Haman hurry to perform Esther's word), but nothing follows from this instruction and Haman is not hurried to do anything. Instead (in 5:6), the king and Haman appear at the banquet and the king again asks Esther what she wants, rhetorically offering her even half his kingdom.

In the standard text, what follows is that Esther asks for a second banquet on the following day (in 5:7–8). The king's agreement to this is not stated but is evident from what Haman then tells his wife: that he alone of the king's subjects was invited to today's banquet and alone is invited to tomorrow's. The king's order in respect of Haman has been forgotten.

At this point the story is interrupted (in Chapter Six) by the unexpected humiliation of Haman and the rewarding of Mordecai for the latter's having saved the king from an assassination plot (in Chapter Two). Chapter Seven continues with the king and Haman attending the second banquet and the king asking Esther a third time what she wants, but without Haman giving any sign of the indignity that he has just suffered.

The other most glaring problem in the narrative occurs in the duplication of the revenge brought by the Jews (in Chapter Nine) against those who would have destroyed them. Once again there is a shorter and longer account. The basic story is that with the king's endorsement, the Jews were able to smite all their enemies by the stroke of the sword (9:5), helped by 'the princes of the provinces and the satraps and the governors and they that did the king's business', though their participation is credited more to a growing fear of Mordecai, whose power is on the rise, than to their respect for the king. Some 500 men are then reported as having been killed in Shushan fortress on 13th Adar. This is followed by two confused accounts. In the first the king is told that Haman's ten sons, who are named, have been killed. He receives this news and marvels at it. He wonders how many more must have been killed in his other provinces, then offers to fulfil any request by Esther and agrees that the ten sons of Haman may be killed the next day, 14th Adar. It appears, therefore, that they are killed twice.

There are passages in the Book of Esther that read so easily in linear form that they disguise the text's dual structure. The most notable example of this appears in Chapter Three, which begins with the promotion of Haman to the premiership of the state. The reasons for this promotion are not given and need unravelling. The text has already identified the individuals who figure most importantly at court: they are the seven chamberlains named in 1:10 (the seven names listed at 1:14 are provincial rulers rather than court officials) and Haman's name does not appear in this list.[5] While the king's appointment of Haman is consistent with the wilfulness associated with absolute power, it appears also to indicate a new phase in the kingship. In the absence of other evidence, we may choose to assume that the seven court officials (Mehuman, Bizzetha, Harvona, Bigtha, Abagtha, Zethar and Carcas) are part of the Persian elite that displaced the older Babylonian ruling class: the unexplained appointment of someone from outside this circle—Haman— may then suggest that Ahasuerus/Xerxes made a political concession to the *ancien régime* (see the Introduction to the First Edition), no doubt under duress.

In addition, the fact that nothing is told us about Haman other than that he was an Agagite and thus a descendant of the Amalekites, the Bible's foremost would-be exterminators of the Jews, might imply that his name was known to the first audience for whom the *Megillah* was written.

Either way, Haman's attitude to the Jews is at once recognisable to anyone: it is the intolerant

nationalism of an indigenous population and its once powerful, now marginalised, ruling caste.

As we have it, Chapter Three is unproblematic. Haman is acutely sensitive to the humiliation, as he sees it, of Persian conquest, and feels further insulted by the lone refusal of Mordecai, a prominent non-Babylonian, to acknowledge his dignity. He therefore seeks and wins the approval of the king for the collective punishment of all Mordecai's people. The four-part structure of Chapter Three reflects this reading: (1) Haman feels dishonoured by Mordecai and determines on the mass destruction of the Jews; (2) Haman asks his friends to decide the most propitious date for the genocide; (3) Haman gets the king to sanction his plan; (4) the king publishes his agreement throughout the empire.

All of this makes for a perfectly credible linear reading—except for one thing: the casting of lots. A more logical chronology would be that Haman took his plan to the king and only determined a date for the slaughter after it had been approved. Instead, the lots are drawn—and not by Haman but by others—before it has been approved. Events, of course, whether in life or in the Bible, do not always move in the most logical order and there can be any number of explanations for why Haman might have gone to the trouble of deciding on a date before ensuring that his scheme had been rubber stamped: perhaps he wanted to sell the king a complete package.

It is reasonable, however, to expect two factors in any storytelling: first, a process of reduction in which only what matters and drives the story forwards is recounted; and second, that a story or part of a story is complete once what has been said is sufficient in itself. This is the problem with Chapter Three. Once Haman has hit upon an auspicious date, we do not need to know anything more, other than that the decision is written down, copied and published. The casting of lots therefore provides a coda to the story of Haman's reaction to Mordecai's habitual insulting of him rather than the halfway point in a longer story. We now know all we need to know: Haman was furious, decided to punish Mordecai and all his race, decided a date for the genocide, and got the royal scribes and couriers to publish this into law.

This gives us reason to treat what follows (3:8–11) as a separate story. Here, Haman is appointed by the king and immediately takes steps to destroy the Jews. In this second account, there is no

5 Acc. to the *Targum Sheni* (Aramaic Second Targum) to *Esther* and the Talmudic Tractate *Megillah*, Haman is in fact identical with Memucan, the seventh of the princes.

snubbing of Haman that we know of; he simply comes to power with a pre-existing hatred of Jews and the desire to annihilate them.

Treated separately, the two stories tell us different things about Haman. In the first—the M text—we learn that Haman is so powerful that he is able to enact laws independently of the king—or, at least, that there is no reason to introduce the king into the narrative because Haman is the prime mover in what follows. In the second—the E text—we learn that Haman has an agenda from the very start of his premiership and that either he was easily able to persuade the king of its merits or that the king was already aware of Haman's desires when appointing him and was either not opposed to them or actually welcomed them.

This latter reading is supported by Mordecai's advice to Esther about not revealing her origins: there is already a dangerous climate of anti-semitism in existence, either in the court or the country at large. In this E version, there was either no snubbing of Haman by Morcedai or the snubbing was not what prompted Haman's proposed slaughter. The E version even suggests that the story of the snubbing was a distraction or an irrelevance and only became the focus of the M account because of the light it shone on Mordecai.

According to the Babylonian Talmud (in Tractate *Baba Bathra* 15a) the text of the Book of Esther was not only included in the canon by the scribes of the Great Assembly but was also redacted by them. What we find odd today (though it seems not to have worried readers in the past) is why those in charge of the text left it in such an unresolved and contradictory state. The answer can only be speculative but we can at least try to see what some of the issues might have been.

In respect of Chapter Five, the problem is one of narrative slippage, where the story-telling is duplicated and the duplications are out of phase with each other. If we take the text literally, for example, we have to suppose that there were two banquets. Perhaps there were. Perhaps the custom of the day was that the greater the favour sought, the greater the number of submissions necessary before the final petition. In purely dramatic terms, however, the first banquet lacks narrative purpose—or at least, none is made explicit—and

it is not unreasonable for us to regard this as unsatisfactory, given the considerable drama of the rest of the book. People 2,500 years ago may have understood why there was a need for two banquets but we do not, or do not have enough evidence for speculating. At the risk of being accused of introducing a modern perspective, we cannot help but be tempted by the view that there was only one banquet and that, as with the feast at the start of the book, we are reading two different narratives, and therefore the writings of two different authors. In the first of these, in just three lines (5:4–6), we are given all we need to know about the lead-up to Esther's real petition; in the second version we are given a more elaborate story, set off by a more ingratiating request that the king and Haman attend Esther's banquet the next day.

Despite the fact that one version calls for an immediate banquet and the other calls for a delayed banquet, the two passages agree on one thing: there was a banquet. What the second version brings is extra detail that the first version lacks and that all the first of the Book of Esther's paired accounts lack.

The second version also adds narrative purpose—and since we have no corroborating evidence, we cannot know whether this is artifice, and therefore an authorial imposition, or a faithful reporting of fact (to the extent that the story has any characters who might be taken as factual). In the second version, the delaying of Esther's banquet until the next day, or some future day, gives the king enough time to discover Mordecai's virtue and start to doubt Haman's. This prepares the ground for Ahasuerus to agree to Esther's petition, which involves nothing less than her unmasking of herself as Jewish, unmasking the shared fate that she will suffer with her people, and unmasking the king's closest adviser as the greatest threat to her and her people's life.

There is one difficulty in disentangling this part of the story into alternative shorter and longer accounts rather than accepting them as linear and sequential: the fact that Haman himself is 'quoted' as referring to two banquets. As against this, it is only in the shorter account that the king orders 'Cause Haman to make haste' and only in the longer version that chamberlains arrive at Haman's house and hasten him to the banquet. In other words, Haman arrives at the first banquet without having to be hurried and is hurried to the second banquet without the king's having made any such order. This makes no sense. The king's request (in the first version) that Haman hurry to the banquet is only satisfied after Haman has been busily occupied elsewhere (in the second version), parading Mordecai round the town and then returning home and mourning his fate—both of which actions are explicitly performed at speed (Haman has to 'make haste' to carry out the king's will in parading Mordecai, and then has to hurry home to avoid further humiliation and seek his wife's advice). Logically, therefore, line 5:5 should appear in the middle of 6:12:

> 6:12 And Mordecai returned to his king's gate.
>
> 5:5 Then the king said: 'Cause Haman to make haste, that it may be done as Esther hath said.'
>
> 6:12 [And] Haman hasted to his house, mourning and having his head covered.

Not only does this gives dramatic point to Haman's unburdening to Zeresh, it also explains why the king's chamberlains have to fetch Haman and bring him to Esther's banquet, which he now no longer wants to attend. Line 5:5 has evidently become detached from its proper place, so there is good reason to want to challenge the text as we find it. Its relocation also enhances the story's dramatic punch if we regard the story only as literature.

Chapter Three offers evidence to suggest that two passages, each independent of the other, have been put together to make a longer, richer narrative. But each passage, both of which relate to Haman's downfall, is disjointed and we have to work hard to make sense of what is written. In combination, the story they tell is no less flawed.

After appointing Haman to the highest office in the empire, for reasons unexplained, it is the king (rather than Mordecai) who then humiliates him, for reasons also unexplained, by making him lead Mordecai in honour round the city and then by misinterpreting his distress over the plot that the king himself has approved.

There is nothing explicit to explain why the king would ask his newly-appointed prime minister to perform the task of stable boy. The king is not honouring Haman by having him lead Mordecai's horse but exploiting him, albeit in accordance with Haman's ill-judged, self-regarding wishes. Although Haman has proposed that the job should be 'delivered to the hand of one of the king's noblest princes' (6:9), his wife and friends see very clearly which way the wind is blowing:

> 6:13 If Mordecai, before whom thou hast begun to fall, be of the seed of the Jews, thou shalt not prevail against him but shalt surely fall before him.

Haman may no longer be in the king's good graces, as those who know him best observe, but the narrative itself does not confirm this. It suggests that Haman may have overreached himself in asking for the king's honoree to be dressed up in 'royal apparel that the king useth to wear' and to be seated on 'the horse that the king rideth upon' and have set 'a royal crown on his head', but nothing states positively that the king has had prior fears of Haman's harbouring dangerous ambitions, or that his anti-Jewish scheme is insane, and no division into M and E versions provides any assistance.

Similarly, nothing explicitly explains the king's anger following Esther's pleas in Chapter Seven. The king was fully aware of Haman's plot against the Jews but not that Esther would be affected by it, because she had not revealed her identity. If it now occurs to him that the killing of the Jews will necessitate the killing of his queen (which is how she presents her predicament), it is only logical to blame Haman if he can establish that Haman knew she was Jewish and said nothing about it. Haman could have known this: he knew that Morcedai was Jewish, may have known that Mordecai visited Esther, and could have worked out the truth of their relationship. But nothing in the text says so.

What then makes the king storm out of the wine feast and into the palace garden? Storming off stage is a classic literary device for illustrating inner turmoil. The text may be suggesting here that the king now suspects that Haman did in fact know more than he has said: that Esther's self-revelation has in turn persuaded him of Haman's capacity for stealth, making him feel newly vulnerable. With Haman and Esther effectively demanding the other's blood, he goes into the garden to consider which to dispose of: the would-be Jew killer or the Jewish infiltrator. We do not know what he decides: the text does not say. But when he returns he finds Haman sprawled across her couch, and that decides it: Haman will have to go. Haman's desperation, however, may indicate that he was genuinely unaware that Esther was

Jewish and had never imagined that she would be caught up in the coming massacre.

We need greater clarity from the narrative and we do not have it. Division into M and E texts is of some help here but only solves a smaller problem: the king's temporary exit from the feast. This interruption—he goes out; he comes back—is unsatisfactory in the same way that the interruption of the casting of lots in Chapter Three is unsatisfactory. It may therefore be serving the same function of separating an M and an E text. If it does, what follows—the king's discovery of Haman on the queen's couch at 7:8—may be a separate E story that has been attached to the main M story to give it extra weight: the king is angry with Haman for presuming to kill Esther and her people and even angrier when he thinks that Haman is also trying to assault her. But the E text strongly suggests—though not to the king—that Haman is guiltless in respect of the queen: he had not meant to harm her either in his plot or on her couch. We can separate the texts but this does not solve the bigger question of explaining the king's thinking or Haman's offence. In addition, it is clear that the editors finally wanted Haman skewered by the irony of his own (relative) innocence, and so the passage has been left in abeyance.

In the case of Chapter Nine, Haman's sons cannot have been killed twice and bright readers can justifiably feel baffled by the duplication and by the failure of the redactors to resolve it.[6] Here, untangling the text does not resolve the problem but may explain why it was left unresolved. What happened in Shushan has to be distinguished from what happened in the other provinces. The Jews in Shushan meted out revenge in the capital on two

days—the 13th and 14th Adar—and celebrated on the 15th. Jews in the provinces completed their attack on 13th Adar and instituted 14th Adar as their annual day of celebration. To bring the provinces in line with the capital, but also to ensure that the capital respected the provinces, Mordecai instructs the entire Jewish population to keep both days as festivals of celebration: the 14th *and* 15th Adar. The redactors of the Great Assembly were not just secular editors but the representatives of Jewish religious authority. Retaining two conflicting accounts of when the ten sons were hanged may have provided them with the bed of uncertainty needed to persuade the entire Jewish community, wherever it was, to keep a two-day festival.[7]

There is one other possible explanation for the survival of the *Megillah*'s two variant texts, and that may have to do with the identity of the authors. Apart from the main body of the text, which is mostly unified, and a couple of places where there seem to be three variations, there are usually only two alternate versions: one that is characteristically briefer and one that is characteristically more detailed and ornamented. This invites us to ask who might have been responsible for each.

Royal courts traditionally sponsored bards or troubadours or dramatists to gather anecdotes and render them in epic, lyric or dramatic form. Shakespeare in this sense was a bard to Queen Elizabeth I. As a story emanating from the court of King Ahasuerus, the Book of Esther may well have been constructed by one such royal poet (or more than one) charged with commemorating the doings of the court, heroising or memorialising its main players, and making events within the royal household available for the wider enjoyment or edification of others, whether of the nobility or the populace.

We know something of how literature of the period was produced in other settings because

---

6 The New Revised Standard Version of the Bible, which includes the Greek version of the Book of Esther, tries to solve the problem of the second hanging by adopting a translation that changes the meaning: '9:13 And Esther said to the king, "Let the Jews be allowed to do the same tomorrow. Also, hang up *the bodies* of Haman's ten sons." 9:14 So he permitted this to be done, and handed over to the Jews of the city the bodies of Haman's sons to hang up.' This suggests that the bodies would be hung up after being massacred, perhaps as a warning, in the way that the decapitated heads of traitors were once put on spikes on London Bridge, but the translator has engaged in supposition and the word 'bodies' does not appear in the Greek. In addition, if the hanging had been meant as a warning rather than a mode of killing, one would expect the Hebrew wording to have specified this.

7 The effort failed, however. Even though the *Megillah* ends with Esther twice confirming Mordecai's instruction, and either Mordecai or the king giving further authority to this religious order, Purim came to be celebrated on one day only: on 15th Adar (known as Shushan Purim) in Jerusalem, in emulation of the custom of Shushan, and—according to the subsequently enacted law—in any other city that was walled when Joshua led the people into the Land of Israel; and on 14th Adar everywhere else.

of the documentation surrounding Aeschylus and *The Persians*, mentioned earlier. *The Persians* is the oldest surviving Greek play and the only surviving Greek tragedy based on contemporary political events. To this extent it is reminiscent of the Book of Esther. In almost every other respect it is utterly different. *The Persians* is poetical and dramatic, highly stylised, full of Aeschylus's difficult language, and designed to be partly spoken and partly sung. It is populated by two main characters (King Darius and his royal mother), a messenger, a ghost (Xerxes) and a chorus of elders. Its deliberate contrivance—which makes it almost impossible to perform today—is partly what won Aeschylus first prize at the Dionysia festival in Athens in 472 BCE.

The Book of Esther, by contrast, appears to have been written in simple demotic Hebrew. It is easy to understand, familiar in its vocabulary and lacking in structural complexity (unless its narrative oddities are an attempt at sophistication). It is as accessible as the popular entertainments of Yiddish theatre a century ago. This is noteworthy in view of the trend in historic literature for poetry—an earlier literary form—to give way to prose as literacy becomes more widespread. Esther, in common with many other books in the Bible, is surprisingly prosaic, suggesting that literacy was long established within the culture from which it sprang.

There is another curiosity here. The standard version of the *Megillah* as we know it in the Bible/ *Tanach* (the Masoretic Text) is not the only version of the Book of Esther. Various Greek translations were produced, the oldest of which (approx. 150– 100 BCE) is known as the Old Greek (OG) and constitutes the version of Esther that appears in the Septuagint (the Greek collection of Jewish biblical writings) and was evidently translated straight from the Hebrew, or a Hebrew, text.

This was the original form of the Greek Esther. It was followed by the 1st-century BCE/CE Alpha-Text (AT), a shorter, alternative Greek version of Esther, which looks less like a revision of the OG and more an independent piece of translation or rewriting, though one that may in places preserve older narrative traditions. Three hundred years later came a stylistic revision by Lucian of Antioch (late 3rd and early 4th century CE) known as the Lucianic Recension. This was much more polished and literary, consistent with other Greek biblical books, but also an attempt to reach out to Hebrew

traditions, and it became an influential text within the Byzantine Church.

The Septuagint reproduces the main thrust of the story but with six quite extensive additions as well as many small but significant textual changes. The first principal addition is a prologue to the story in which Mordecai, described as a great man already serving in the king's court, has a dream. In the dream he hears thunder and explosions and sees two huge roaring dragons preparing to fight, as well as the nations of the world preparing to join battle to subdue 'the righteous nation'. The righteous nation is terrified and cries out to God, after which it is delivered by sunlight pouring from a tiny spring that becomes a great river. Mordecai wakes and tries to make sense of what he takes to be a portent of God's will. The prologue is matched by an epilogue in which Mordecai interprets what he now sees as the fulfilment of that portent: the spring that became a river is identified with Esther, the two dragons are Haman and himself, the nations are those who would have destroyed the Jews, and the righteous nation is Israel. (For other examples, see Additional Notes, page 17.)

These additions are intriguing because they recall the folk culture of Babylon and Persian neo-Babylon, which was rife with legends about fairies, monsters and demons. These ranged, over the course of more than 1,500 years of Akkadian literature, from ancient epics such as the creation myth *Enûma Eliš*, about the victory of Marduk over the water-chaos dragon Tiamat, to later prophetic texts, incantations, histories, myths, fables and comedies. A surprising amount of this has survived, at least in fragments, and some of the best examples occur in stories written or revised by and for the Jewish community in Babylon. Some of these are canonical: the second Jewish creation myth in *Genesis* (magic serpent persuades Eve to commit the first sin) and the Book of Jonah (recalcitrant prophet gets eaten and then vomited by giant fish).[8] The rest

8   Among other canonical examples, apart from references to the idols of other nations, are the teraphim and nephilim (in Genesis); the destroyer (in Exodus and elsewhere); the kherubim (in Exodus); Balaam's talking donkey (in Numbers); the four-winged creatures (in the Book of Ezekiel); the behemoth and leviathan (in the Book of Job); the four allegorical monsters (the lion with an eagle's wings, the bear-like creature, the leopard with four wings and four heads, and the creature with iron teeth and ten horns) that come out of the sea and threaten the world (in The Book of Daniel); and angels (various).

are Jewish demon writings that were preserved by being translated into Greek (whether from Hebrew or Aramaic originals) and incorporated into the Septuagint but not included in the Jewish canon—hence 'deuterocanonical'—such as *Bel and the Dragon*[9] (Daniel kills a Babylonian dragon-deity by feeding it *matzot*—barley cakes—that cause it to explode when eaten) and the *Book of Tobit* (angel helps son of a man blinded by bird droppings to use the entrails of a fish that tries to swallow him (a) to drive away a demon that has so far killed seven men before they can consummate their marriage to the woman he wishes to marry, and (b) to cure his father's blindness).

Apart from the story of Eve and the serpent and the Book of Jonah, Jewish redactors did not like demon stories, even though such stories might include within them affirmations of the greater power and virtue of God. In the first part of *Bel and the Dragon*, for example, Daniel proves that an idol (Bel) worshiped by King Cyrus is a false deity, and he goes on to kill a dragon, for which he is thrown into a lions' den (as before, in the Book of Daniel, Chapter 6) but is saved by a prophet, causing the king to proclaim 'Great art thou, O Lord God of Daniel, and there is none other besides thee.' In *Tobit*, the blinded Tobit prays to God for death; before their first wedding night, his son and daughter-in-law pray to God for life; and when they all meet and Tobit's sight is restored, they all give thanks to God. Similarly, in the Greek version of the Book of Esther, after 4:17 in the *Megillah*, when Haman's plot is revealed, first Mordecai prays to God at length, then Esther prays to God at even greater length, and both use formulas of supplication still employed in Jewish prayer today. The Greek text has numerous other references to God as an active force in the world, in stark contrast to the Jewish *Megillah*, in which God goes unmentioned.

According to tradition, translation of Judaism's canonical texts into Greek began in the early third century BCE on the orders of the Egyptian king, Ptolemy II Philadelphus, and was complete by the late second century BCE. Tradition also holds that the translation of the fundamental texts—the Five Books of Moses—was strikingly rigorous and consistent, while translation of the later texts was more wayward. In respect of how the story of

Esther was formalised, we may assume that there was a certain amount of interplay between the Jewish redactors and their Greek counterparts. At the same time, those who formalised Judaism's canonical texts are customarily said to have exercised tight editorial control: they had access to the Greek additions but they excluded them. In the case of the Book of Esther, they had the option of re-writing the Esther story as a religious morality tale—using their own or other, non-Greek material—but they chose not to. Thus, although the *Megillah* ends by quoting Mordecai's call for a two-day festival in recognition of the Jews' salvation, the Jewish version is explicitly historical and temporal.

There are two possible reasons. First, Esther ends with the statement that 'the history of the king's power and strength, and the account of the greatness of Mordecai, whom the king promoted, are recorded in the *Book of the Chronicles of the Kings of Media and Persia*.' Judaism had its own *Book of Chronicles* (*Divrei HaYamim*) which provides a history of the biblical southern kingdom (Judea), focusing on the role of Jerusalem as Judaism's pre-exilic religious centre and largely ignoring Jewish life as it was lived in Egypt, the wilderness, the northern kingdom (Israel), Nineveh and Babylon. It ends with Cyrus inviting the Jewish people to return to Jerusalem and licensing the rebuilding of the Temple (completed under Darius). The later story of Esther is therefore outside its timespan and editorial remit; it follows that its origins must lie elsewhere.

Since the Book of Esther refers twice to the *Book of the Chronicles of the Kings of Media and Persia*, now lost, it is fair to assume that the text as we have it may have been taken over verbatim or largely verbatim from here instead. That is to say, although it records a Jewish victory, *Esther* may not in its origins be a Jewish but a Persian story, with no editorial or religious agenda except as the record of an affair of state. If this is so, the Jewish editors imported into the scriptural canon an authentic external document—a court manuscript—and were scrupulous in not ascribing or adding to it religious content that, as a Persian text, it was not competent to provide.

There is a second and equally plausible explanation for the absence of religious references in *Esther*. When God appears as a presence in other Neo-Babylonian biblical works, he acts to balance the malign force of various magical creatures that

9   The story appears as Chapter 14 in the extended Greek version of the Book of Daniel.

intervene in the world. To this extent his status is diminished: he may be the most powerful and kindly of these other-worldy entities but he is not unique. This is essentially the theology of Zoroastrianism, the religion inspired by the sixth-century BCE Persian mystic Zoroaster (Zarathustra), with whom all the principal Persian rulers of Babylon are thought to have been personally and formally associated. Zoroastrianism posited a single, beneficent and ultimately omnipotent god, Ahura Mazdā,[10] constantly preoccupied with having to suppress evil spirits that provoked and tried to undermine him.

Zoroastrian belief can be seen as a projection of Persia's politics: the endless struggles of Cyrus, Cambyses, Darius and Xerxes to keep down other nations—Egyptians, Greeks, Medes, Babylonians, etc—as well as internal rebels. This was a template that Babylonian Jews, displaced from their land and untroubled by imperial ambition, had no reason to share. Since 597 BCE, their politics had been a matter solely of self-management; as a nation in exile they were at the mercy of their captors. Unlike the Persians, the Jewish template was therefore one of total dependency on a higher power, whether temporal or spiritual. This is important in how the Jewish view of God developed and diverged from the religious views of politically more autonomous neighbours.

Political circumstances further complicated Jewish thinking. Magical relativism was imprinted into Babylonian culture: ungovernable occult forces were a constant threat and human beings had no choice but to try and placate them. To this chaos of fear, the Persians brought a less terrifying idea: that of stratified discord. Within Zoroastrianism, Ahura Mazdā occupies a higher realm; evil spirits—the minions of the evil Angra Mainyu or Ahriman—occupy a lower one; and the two sides play out their conflicts in the earthly middleground where human beings live. Humans get involuntarily caught up in their battles, either directly or as part of the collateral damage, but need only focus their efforts on propitiating the one higher god.

In spite of their Zoroastrianism, the Achaemenid rulers whom the Jews lived under all adopted a policy of religious pluralism: from Cyrus to Xerxes, conquered people were allowed and even encouraged to worship their own gods. This tolerance dampened dissent and made possible the social stability that powered Neo-Babylon's massive economic renaissance. Babylon's Jews benefited greatly from this but also knew that the policy of tolerance could be reversed at any moment and by no means had the assent of Babyon's indigenous elite or, in particular, its priestly class—*pro tem* less powerful than hitherto but always looking for an opportunity to rise again. As captives, the Jews had nowhere to escape to and, unlike other nations, no access to military force, which is what makes the conclusion of the Book of Esther story so distinct. They were, moreover, easily identifiable as religious non-conformists: in this respect, Mordecai is acutely aware of Esther's vulnerability, and of his own, and of the people's. As Haman says to Ahasuerus (3:8): 'There is a certain people scattered abroad and dispersed among the peoples in all the provinces of thy kingdom and their laws are diverse from those of every people, neither keep they the king's laws. Therefore it profiteth not the king to suffer them.'

The Jews' best interest lay, therefore, in keeping a low profile, which meant overt obedience to the king, even at risk of offending the local upper classes (as Mordecai offended Haman). Any perception of divided loyalty had to be resisted. The absence of God in the Book of Esther is thus an illustration of a strategic silence. In this narrative, the highest force in the land is the king and everything that happens is the product of his assent. It is Ahasuerus who has to be propitiated, first by Haman who offers to put ten thousand talents of silver into the king's treasuries, and then more powerfully by Esther who fasts for three days, hosts a banquet (or two banquets), employs her charisma and beauty, weeps and entreats, calls on the king's powers—his legal mechanisms, royal scribes, fast messengers, and horses from the royal stud—to reinforce his authority, and organises a blood bath in the king's name to prove his military might.

The most patent explanation for the mostly secular character of the Book of Esther is, finally, that it records the Jews' victory over Haman as a direct consequence of 'the king's commandment and his decree' and of no other agency (other than Mordecai's promptings and Esther's machinations). In that sense, the *Megillah* is a tribute or testimonial to the temporal power. This is what the king in question would have demanded, what anyone reading the story would have expected, and what anyone associated with the court and attentive to his or her own survival would have set out to write.

Since the book makes several references to scribes, it is possible that scribes—those referred to or others—were involved in its production, either directly and creatively or in a merely secretarial capacity. Jewish tradition takes no position on this. Tradition suggests, however, as already noted, that the book was written by Mordecai on his own or by Mordecai and Esther. In the absence of evidence, it is impossible to comment on this with confidence but the presence of two alternative versions of the story, as discussed above, does suggest dual authorship. The tone of the two voices has already been referred to: the first brief and unornamented, the second more detailed and florid.

More significantly, the second voice tends to contain inside information more likely to have been known to Esther, or an Esther character, than to Mordecai, or a Mordecai character: these include details of the housing and grooming of virgins for the king's pleasure in Chapter Two, of other events that took place in the king's palace to which a Mordecai would not have been privy, of the wording of conversations with Hathach (Chapter Four) and Ahasuerus (Chapter Five *et seq*), and of the take-up of the king's revised edict in the provinces rather than just in Shushan (Chapter Nine). In the same way, the more perfunctory versions suggest less first-hand knowledge.

For convenience, therefore, though this is only fanciful, we have labelled the two versions 'Mordecai' and 'Esther' or M and E.

The M text is more concerned with authority, reputation and the excellence of majesty, and where there is a choice it is always the M text that appears first. It is M that announces the scope of Ahasuerus's reign, the monumentality of his half-year feast, and the nobility and military prowess of those who attended the feast and whose entry into the city would have been marked by ceremonial honours. It is M that provides information about Esther, gives credence to her exceptional allure, and concentrates on those of her actions that have a decisive effect. The E text invariably follows, providing background and colour, and in 8:5–6 introducing the *Megillah*'s

only moment of poetry. We might regard M here as representative of the more objective historiography of emergent Athenian culture, Thucydidean in its detachment and ambition, and E as representative of an older, more subjective Persian tradition of storytelling.

In some parts of the *Megillah* the story is carried not by two texts but by one. Some readers may regard these solo passages as detached from the M/E polarity or even as evidence of its absence or non-existence; others may read them as essentially M or essentially E. It is the view of this essay that each may indeed be either M or E, but that without more information, it is impossible to say which of the two they are. The long-winded account of how the king's second decree was published in the provinces (8:9–14) repeats the same literary formula that was used to recall the publishing of the first decree (3:12–15), including the same repetitive tripartite structure. This detail and repetition may reflect the conventional flourishes of formal records or the garrulousness or fastidiousness of the reporter. To choose one interpretation rather than another, however, let alone ascribing garrulousness to E and fastidiousness to M, is unsafe and means resorting to stereotypes: literary stereotypes and even gender stereotypes.

In some passages, for example, we may think we hear overtones of a Polonius. When Mordecai is reported as putting on sackcloth and coming to the king's gate (4:2), a caveat is attached, explaining that Mordecai does not go beyond the king's gate because 'none might enter within the king's gate clothed in sackcloth'. This can be read as the writings of a court bureaucrat for whom etiquette is all important. Similarly, the way in which Ahasuerus's ignorance of Esther's origins is framed—that Esther had 'not yet made known her kindred nor her people, as Mordecai had charged her' (2:20)—can be read not just as a neutral piece of information about what the king knew but as a comment on Esther's deference and obedience to Mordecai. Both texts are in that sense self-serving: the first remark (on etiquette) is self-excusing and a little pompous, the second remark (on Esther) is a compliment on the control that Mordecai still exercises over the young queen. If this second remark is an M text, it functions as a condescending observation on Esther's compliance as Mordecai's still dutiful step-daughter, but it is not necessarily this. The examples might just as well be by Esther, or an Esther-type scribe, in the first case priding herself on her awareness of court protocols and in the second case confirming the queen's (or the writer's) sense of discretion.

In short, without a balancing text, we cannot tell whether these solo, uncontested examples are written from a female or male perspective, or by an ingenue or a court habitué. The first example may indicate a girlish nervousness about protocol; the second may reveal Esther's (or an E's) rather than Mordecai's (or an M's) pride in the queen's piety. Nor is there evidence that these are even the writings of a younger or older person. That the story is about a young Esther does not means that a young Esther, or a young E, wrote it. The portrait of Esther is what one would expect of a literary composition and may be the contrivance of an Esther when older or of a more experienced third party.

With this warning in mind, we have to work very hard to resist the interpretation of Polonian pettiness. At the start of Chapter Nine, for example, we might consider that the narrative is interrupted twice and then delayed twice for no reason except pedantry. The basic sentence runs as follows:

> 9:1 Now in the twelfth month which is the month Adar on the thirteenth day of the same when the king's command and his decree drew near to be put in execution, 9:2 the Jews gathered together in their cities throughout all the provinces of King Ahasuerus to lay hand on such as sought their hurt, and no man could withstand them for the fear of them was fallen upon all the peoples.

Although straightforward, this sentence is broken into twice just before 9:2, first with this:

> in the day that the enemies of the Jews hoped to have rule over them

and then by this:

> whereas it was turned to the contrary that the Jews had rule over them that hated them.

The two additions are redundant: instead of driving the drama forwards, they slow it down; and in any case we already have these facts. The action is then held up further by no fewer than three character references. All we need to know is what line 9:5 says:

> 9:5 And the Jews smote all their enemies with the stroke of the sword and with slaughter and destruction and did what they would unto them that hated them.

Instead, we have to wait for:

> 9:3 And all the princes of the provinces and the satraps and the governors and they that did the king's business helped the Jews because the fear of Mordecai was fallen upon them

and:

> 9:4 For Mordecai was great in the king's house and his fame went forth throughout all the provinces,

and:

> for the man Mordecai waxed greater and greater.

We might be forgiven for reading into at least two of these additions an M voice that gets louder from 9:20. From here to the end of the *Megillah*, it is Mordecai who attracts all the attention—as the king's Number Two, the Jews' Number One and no longer the queen's step-father but her joint-equal father:

> 9:29 Then wrote Queen Esther *the daughter of* Abihail (*and of Mordecai the Jew*).

It is Mordecai who now takes on Ahasuerus's job of sending out orders to the provinces, apparently without reference upwards, almost overshadowing the king in his zeal and new-found importance. Lest he put himself at risk, Mordecai tactically acknowledges (10:3) that he was 'second unto King Ahasuerus' but then basks in the fact that he too is now memorialised alongside the king in the imperial *Book of Chronicles* and that he is adored by his people. Both within the events of the story and the structure of the language, Mordecai completely displaces the book's eponymous heroine.

We might therefore be forgiven also for discerning a tension, even a competitiveness, here between Mordecai and Esther in the way that the story oscillates between M passages and E passages (if this is how we choose to read them). In Chapter

Nine, the account of events in Shushan where Mordecai is now in effective control seems to be carried by M texts that favour Mordecai but is interrupted by E texts that stress what is happening further afield, and do so in a way that seems to challenge Mordecai's monopoly. An M text at 9:15, for example, talks about the killings in Shushan on 14th Adar; an E text at 9:16 then ignores this information and talks about the killings in the provinces the day before. Similarly, an M text at 9.18 stresses that the Jews in Shushan rampaged for two days and celebrated on the third while an E text at 9:19 determines that provincial Jews rampaged for only one day and celebrated on the second.

This putative contest between M texts and E texts is not just a matter of arguing about who dictates the public record: it is personal as well. At 8:3, an M text writes off Esther's pleas to the king as girlish weeping until a lengthier E text at 8:4–6 counters by quoting the psalmic lyricism of what she actually said. Similarly, the implied sequitur that 'The Jews smote all their enemies with the stroke of the sword' (9:5) because 'Mordecai was great in the king's house' (9:4) is contradicted at 9:13 by an E text that attributes the killings in Shushan not to Mordecai's power but to Esther's entreaties. More pointedly, the M text at 9.4 ('For Mordecai was great in the king's house and his fame went forth throughout all the provinces') appears to be challenged by the altogether more ambivalent E text substitution: 'for the man Mordecai waxed greater and greater'—'the man', not 'the king's new deputy'.

In literary terms, the E texts deploy the theme of reversal against the theme of celebrity. In an M text at 9:20, Mordecai is credited with converting local one-day Purim celebrations into an empire-wide two-day event—a clever political initiative meant to knit Shushanite and provincial Jews together—but in a corresponding E text (9:25), the main credit is shifted to Esther for having persuaded the king to reverse Haman's plan. In the same way, one of the interruptions at the start of Chapter Nine ('whereas it was turned to the contrary that the Jews had rule over them that hated them') reminds the reader of Esther's role, not Mordecai's, in reversing Ahasuerus's decision and bringing matters to a happy conclusion.

The object of this essay has not been to determine whether the Esther story is a real historical event or a folktale, as all scholars now hold it to be. In the absence of definitive evidence, it might be either or a mixture of both. For our purposes, the rootedness of the story in reality or fable is immaterial; what matters here is how the narrative was constructed and what function it performed, and that requires an understanding of the techniques of literary criticism. For example, the language used to describe Mordecai in the ninth and tenth chapters has conventionally been thought of as respectful, as befitting a heroic leader who saw an opportunity and a threat, took appropriate action in both cases and had the gratification of seeing both his interventions succeed, to his own and his people's considerable advantage. If we take this view, the idea of rival M texts and E texts, of competition between Esther and Mordecai, and of the narrative as nuanced and coded has to be dismissed—but that also means choosing not to see what is in front of us. To treat the text as editorially neutral—even to treat it as hagiographic or heroising—is to blind oneself to what actually appears.

Even if one ignores the new interpretations that literary analysis offers, we are still left with sufficient evidence of variant texts, repetitions, inconsistencies, changes of emphasis and stylistic alternatives to reveal the book not as a seamless work but a patchwork quilt. We know as a matter of historic record, in any case, that additional material—the Greek additions and changes—were excluded from the canonic text and we can now speculate on why. Much of the Greek material seems to have been offered up in order to give the *Megillah* the religious dimension that it otherwise lacks.

This was evidently not welcome to the editors, for two reasons at least. One has already been discussed: the wish to preserve the secularity of the story as a homage to the ruling powers. The other relates to the source. From the period when the events in *Esther* appear to have taken place to the period when the story was redacted, the Persian empire was troubled by various Greek city states that were also at war with each other. Cyrus had conquered the region of Ionia in 547. Persian rule led in 499 to an Ionian revolt that, though not without some success (notably the destruction of the Persian capital at Sardis), was finally put down in 493. Darius then sent two invasionary forces to conquer Greece, the first in 492 only partially successful, the second in 490 ending in Persian defeat by the Athenians at the Battle of Marathon. In retaliation, Xerxes launched a second invasion in 480 that succeeded on land but was routed at sea. Persian ambitions were finally denied in 479 when the Greeks destroyed both the Persian army and its fleet, and by extension ensured the rise of what is now regarded as a more purely Greek culture and a Western civilisation based on Greek rather than Persian or Perso-Greek foundations. The Persians continued to be driven back during the 470s and hostilities were finally brought to an end, apparently by treaty, around 449.

It is self-evident that there was much at stake in relations between Persians and Greeks. It is also evident that while much of the Jewish world lived in areas under Greek rule or Greek influence, Jewish authority itself continued to operate from a base that was under Persian control. According to Jewish tradition, the Great Assembly, if it ever existed as an entity (which is now doubted), was instituted by Ezra and centred on Jerusalem after Cyrus gave the Jews of Babylon freedom to return to Judea. The Assembly, or the authority of its supposed 120 sages, spanned several centuries and among its earliest members was Zerubabel (meaning 'born in Babylon'),[11] the grandson of Jehoiachin, the penultimate king of Judah, and the man credited with leading the first Jews back to Jerusalem.[12] Zerubabel was appointed first governor of Judea under Persian rule by Darius and completed the rebuilding of the Temple that Cyrus had sanctioned. Judea remained a Persian province for two hundred years, from 539 to 332, when it was taken over by the Macedonian Greeks under Alexander. In all that time, the religious and political authorities in Jerusalem were aware that their continued existence in Judea was on sufferance and that just as the Jews had been allowed to return by the Persians, they could also be transported back to Babylon again at any time.

We therefore have reason to read a measure of political caution into all writings of this period. While it is clear that a substantial proportion of Persia's Jewish population had already become hellenised long before Judea became a Greek

11   The name is traditionally spelled Zerubbabel in English but there is no etymological reason for the second b.
12   Mordecai is also said to have been among those who returned to Jerusalem, but nothing in the final verses of *Esther* supports this.

client state, the authorities in Jerusalem had a vested interest in not favouring Greek ideas if there was any risk that by doing so they might destabilise their own status quo. This must go some way to explaining the reluctance to include Greek materials in the Jewish canon.

As noted (page 9), there are significant differences between the Hebrew (Masoretic) Book of Esther and the Greek versions (principally the Septuagint); in fact, Esther is one of the most textually divergent books in the Bible, giving added force to the argument against seeing the book as uniform and harmonious. The differences concern not just wording but length, theology, style, and narrative framing. Most evidently, the Greek Esther contains six large additions not found in the Hebrew text:

Addition A: Mordecai's Dream (Prologue)
    Mordecai receives a prophetic dream that fore-shadows dark events. It is expressed in strongly apocalyptic imagery and is explicitly theological.
Addition B: The Royal Decree
    The full text of Haman's edict. This portrays Jews as lawless and dangerous, and articulates Haman's political motivations.
Addition C: Prayers of Mordecai and Esther
    These are lengthy, emotional prayers to God. In her prayer, Esther explicitly rejects her royal status and pagan surroundings, and adopts a deep penitential tone.
Addition D: Esther Before the King
    This provides a dramatic expansion of Esther's entreaties to the king, after which God directly intervenes to change the king's heart, Esther faints from fear of what will happen, and angels (it is implied) appear to hold her up.
Addition E: The Counter–Decree
    The full text of the king's second decree in which God is explicitly credited with delivering the Jews from harm.
Addition F: Interpretation of the Dream (Epilogue)
    Mordecai interprets the opening dream and God is again explicitly identified as the agent of salvation.

The additions increase the length of the Greek Esther by about half.

In the Greek Esther, God is named and active; the narrative refers to prayer and repentance and carries a religious purpose that aligns it with other biblical texts. By contrast, in both the M and E versions of the Hebrew Esther, God is absent. Neither character talks about prayer or prophecy or religious law. When Mordecai learns that the Jewish people are to be wiped out, he rips his clothes, puts on sackcloth and ashes, goes out into the middle of the city and wails, and Jews in the king's other provinces do the same, fasting and weeping and wailing. We do not we hear any invocations to the Deity from them, however. Mordecai and the people are in distress and they respond formulaically, but they do not pray. Nor does Esther. Her immediate thought is procedural: she worries about the protocol of going to entreat the king when he hasn't asked for her recently, and then has Mordecai organise a three-day hunger strike for her as an act of appeasement. For both of them—and this passage is the longest one in the *Megillah* where it is impossible to tell who wrote what—the text emphasises human agency and strategy, and both Mordecai and Esther operate perfectly happily within that framework.

Religious commentators—Jewish commentators, anyway—have always written this off as a textual anomaly. They hold that the main characters must have been powerfully devout and God-fearing for them to have wanted to resist genocide, and for the subsequent redactors to want to include them in the canon of Jewish biblical writings. It is just that the text does not say so, for reasons much argued over. But the Masoretic text is far more compelling if we accept it at face value, as a story that tells us something about the Jews' religiously-detached mindset at the time of the Persian ascendancy. Jews undoubtedly saw themselves (and were seen by others) as a distinct ethnic group, and a vulnerable one, but had lost touch with their faith, which was geographically rooted in Judea, the land from which they had been forcibly displaced. They now lived at close quarters with a group whose beliefs, also geographically specific, were alien to them and what we may be seeing is evidence that close proximity to other people's gods and superstitions made them sceptical about all religion, while at the same becoming partially assimilated to unusual Babylonian practices— both situations very familiar to us today. We know from what historians have written about those members of the Jewish community who returned to Jersualem when allowed to by Cyrus that they took only the slimmest of religious knowledge with them, and that Judaism had to be reinvented. That, precisely, is what Ezra has always been credited for, and it explains Mordecai's cynicism. Had he been less disdainful of authority and more civil, he would have bowed down to Haman and saved himself and everyone else a lot of trouble. And yet, alone of all the king's servants, he not only found it impossible to honour the leading figure in Shushan's ancien regime by bowing to him (3:2), he could not even stand up or move out of the way for him a short while after (5:9), even though this meant disobeying the king's orders. Given what followed, it might have been better if he had, but then we would not have had this book of salvation literature. The Lord works in mysterious ways . . .

Mordecai's contempt for class privilege and social snobbery reads well to us, as it must have done for the audience for whom the *Megillah* was originally written. Along with the implicit attack on the sexism of the first chapter, it makes the Book of Esther one of the first liberation manifestos in history, and one that still has not received full recognition. From it, Mordecai emerges not just as the leading Jewish figure of his day but as the foremost champion of equal rights, reflecting a cynicism about Babylonian culture that would have been widely shared and that resonated with his constituency. For the Alexandrian audience, however, he gets converted into a pious figure, confrontational when faced with arrogance and cultural bigotry but motivated by Haman's insult to God, rather than by pride or social defiance.

So we might say that the Book of Esther was not originally meant as a book about religious salvation in which the authors simply forgot to say anything about God: it is a book about social issues and how two very different figures—Mordecai and Esther— handled their community's precarious status, took matters into their own hands and, without ever resorting to violence, played the system against itself. (The violence came afterwards, as payback.)

This was not how it was read 250 years later, after Judaism had been successfully reestablished in Jerusalem by Ezra and his successors and had expanded into the Greek diaspora. This can be confusing because we talk of the 'Greek' versions as if the revisions were the products of Greeks. That's not unreasonable, in view of the fact that the Septuagint eventually came to be the preferred biblical text of the Early Christians, many of whom spoke Greek, even in Rome, before Latin became dominant. The fact that Greek versions of the Bible could be used by non-Jews, and that Greek culture was associated with paganism and assimilation, made the Septuagint eventully appear a threat to religious purity. Its divergences in wording, theology and content from the Masoretic text, and the fact that the New Testament quoted from it extensively rather than from the Masoretic text, also led the rabbinate to regard it as suspect and taboo.

The authorship of the Greek texts can be traced back, however, not to Greeks but to Greek-speaking Jews and to Alexandria, which Alexander the Great had founded in 331 BCE to control Egypt, after winning it from the Persians. Under the Ptolemy dynasty that succeeded Alexander, the port city became a vital administrative hub, a center of learning and home to large communities of Greek and Jewish immigrants, for whom Greek was the lingua franca and Hellenism the prevailing culture. Jewish residents continued to observe the laws and customs that had been revived in Judea but they no longer spoke Hebrew frequently or fluently, and needed scriptural materials—the *Torah* and the prophetic writings—in a language they could understand. This led them to translate the *Tanach* into Greek and, in doing so, to offer an editorial reworking of biblical tradition that reflected their own Hellenistic cultural milieu and their view of earlier texts.

Thus it was that the Book of Esther was reframed into something unambiguously religious, having never been this before. As a result of the Alexandrian translators' additions, we are left with a picture of what seemed, in the third century BCE, to be a recognisably Jewish environment, an image of what third-century Jews thought Judaism had looked like in the fifth century or what it should have looked like.

It was also made into a more Hellenistic work. The Greek editors seem to have seen the Hebrew text of Esther as a primitive literary work, with unexpected repetitions and reversals and a confused sense of time. What they wanted to show was that Jewish culture could compete with Greek culture—that it was no less sophisticated—and so they added long formal speeches and verbatim transcriptions of Jewish prayers, all couched in a more urbane, more respectful tone: a new politesse. That does not mean, however, that they took liberties with the Hebrew version, as is

sometimes suggested by scholars whose casual generalisations do not take care to exclude the six new passages. The original text was left to stand in exactly the same condition as it was found, and for a very good reason. As a piece of writing, the Book of Esther is not a literary creation: it illustrates a social dynamic. The narratives are tight and economic; there are plays on words; and events at court are relayed in the language of satire rather than deference because, it would appear, the Jews of those days were naturally more oppositional and ill-at-ease, as Mordecai was, and less respectful towards their host culture.

Nor is it obvious that the Greek translation has a more elevated, more refined register than the Hebrew version is capable of. In defence of such a claim, it is common to compare part of line 3:4 in the Masoretic text ('To see whether Mordecai's words would stand') unfavourably with the OG 'To see whether Mordecai's λόγος would endure', but this is to load Greek with cultural assumptions that only speak to the prejudices of the observer. The word דבר (*davar*) in the Hebrew phrase— לִרְאוֹת הֲיַעַמְדוּ דִּבְרֵי מָרְדֳּכַי (*lirot haya'amdu dibrei Mordecai*—contains exactly the same multiple connotations as λόγος (*logos*): word, thing, matter, business. When a scholar says that *logos* elevates *davar* to 'rationale'/'claim'/'stated position', this is nonsense. The same wishful thinking exists in a common reception of the Old Greek version of Esther 4:8.[13] The Greek, it is said, may not change the words but it 'expands' the manner of reporting: Mordecai 'entrusts' (ἔδωκεν) the document to Hathach, and has him 'charge' (ἐντείλασθαι) Esther to go in to the king. 'Nothing new happens,' it is said, 'but the speech-act is cast in administrative language, the sort used for petitions, instructions, and reports'. Not so—or not more so than has already been observed of the Masoretic text in the dual authorship model proposed in these pages. To say otherwise suggests only that the speaker has an inflated regard for Greek culture.

For some later rabbinical commentators, the six passages inserted by the Greek editors, and their reliance on their own Greek translations rather than the Hebrew originals, are evidence

13 [Mordecai] also *gave* [Hathach] the copy of the writing of the decree that was given out in Susa to destroy them, to show it to Esther, and to declare it to her, and to *charge* her to go in to the king, to make supplication to him and to make request before him, for her people.

of bowdlerisation, a stripping of authenticity that reminds us of how Shakespeare's plays were rewtitten in the early nineteenth century to make them more accessible and to clarify their supposed moral messages for younger audiences. The rabbis found this troubling. In Jewish law, adding to a sacred text is no less heinous than reducing it[14] and *Talmud* (*Sanhedrin* 59a) expands this injunction to cover oral interpretations as well. Making too much of God was bad theology because the Divine presence should be inferred, not spelled out. Using Greek upstaged the sacred language of Hebrew and rendered it secondary. Narrative clarity risked blocking off the possibility of ambiguous midrashic explanations. And making Scripture available to all violated the norms of holiness. In another passage from the *Talmud, Megillah* 9a, there is specific discomfort with translation into Greek, rather than other languages, but even when the rabbis allowed it, they did so only for translating a Torah scroll, not for other books of the Bible, which they said could only be in Hebrew.

How radical were the Alexandrians? Modern scholarship asks us to take care not to exaggerate the editorial challenge that their versions represent. Rabbinic leaders in Jerusalem came to regard the Alexandrians as having gone too far in adapting inherited texts to a new cultural environment, but the Alexandrians themselves regarded their work as faithful transmission rather than innovation, and themselves as authorised mediators of holy tradition. To say, therefore, that their work offered a self-conscious, reflective critique of the Hebrew *Megillah* suggests an intellectual distance and corrective intention that would not have been recognised by them and is simply modern and anachronistic.

But maybe such a view is too cautious. The Alexandrians were hugely literate; the *Mishna* quoted above also records the origin of the 'Septuagint' label: the legend of how 'King Ptolemy of Egypt assembled seventy-two Elders from the Sages of Israel, put them into seventy-two separate rooms . . . and asked each of them "Write for me a translation of the *Torah* of Moses, your teacher."' The story continues:

> The Holy One, Blessed be He, placed wisdom in the heart of each and every one, and they all agreed to one common understanding. Not only did they all translate the text correctly, they all introduced the same changes into the translated text.

The legend of the seventy-two translators would have been written down in the fourth or fifth century CE in the Babylonian Talmud, and it is framed to highlight the translators' piety and the protection of the *Torah* by Divine intervention. But a very similar story of seventy-two sages translating the *Torah* for Ptolemy II Philadelphus appears in a letter written in the second or first century BCE, possibly by a court official using the name Aristeas, of whom nothing is known and which may have been false. In other words, the Talmud canonises a story that it presents as miraculous but which depends on an earlier Hellenistic legend.

Taking the story out of its Talmudic context, what is evident is that there was a vibrant literary culture among Alexandrian Jews and one that must have buzzed with ideas, however conformist *Megillah* 9a later depicted it to be. We have every reason to think there was as much intellectual energy within the community as there was in the communities of Sura and Pumbedita, the two academies in what is now Iraq that were responsible for compiling the Babylonian Talmud. The only difference is that we do not have an Alexandrian Talmud to prove it, and that is because Jewish life in Alexandria was not built around institutions of learning, in the way that those in Mesopotamia were, and because there was more engagement, and a more respectful engagement, with the culture of the host nation: Hellenism. Within that world, however, it seems improbable that some Alexandrians did not think they were doing something new and bold in revising biblical works and that there was every reason for such revision—even that there existed something not unlike what we might today call a critical engagement, albeit that engagement did not exist in the self-conscious way that criticism operates today.

There is one other area of disagreement revealed by this alternative definition of dual authorship in the *Megillah*—that of the competing Hebrew and Greek voices rather than the M and E voices—and that is in the character

14 You shall not add to the word that I command you, nor take from it, that you may keep the commandments of the Lord your God that I command you (Deuteronomy 4:2).

portrayals. In the Masoretic text, Esther is astute, courageous but restrained; her Greek self is more fearful, pious and emotional. The Hebrew Mordecai is a wily court insider and strategist, a cynic, even a schemer; in Greek he is more of a prophetic figure, a dreamer, and a religious intercessor. King Ahasuerus is different too: the Hebrew text depicts him as weak, impulsive and easily manipulated. The Greek version of him is still flawed, but more morally reflective— willingly to be guided by divine influence in the way that the Ninevites were when confronted by Jonah's angry warnings.

Here, for our purposes, the question of dual authorship risks becoming doubly complicated by the possibility that the Alexandrian text offers pairs of voices with different inflexions and, by extension, different messages from those embedded in the Masoretic text. Fortunately, the idea can be dismissed at once. First, the possibility of different inflexions only applies if one rolls the six additions into the rest of the text, so that the Old Greek version reads as all of a piece, and we have no reason to do this. It may be that the Alexandrians were finally putting down on parchment a centuries-old oral tradition regarding the godliness of Mordecai and Esther, but there is no evidence for saying this. Some scholars think the additions may reflect earlier liturgical or interpretive motifs rather than being pure invention, but this too is only speculative.

Second, dividing the text into two voices and identifying those voices as M for Mordecai and E for Esther is only illustrative of a difference in tone. We have no knowledge of how the text was written, or when, or by whom, and the use of the two main characters' names, while suggestive, is no more than a convenient labelling device.

In saying that, I am aware that I am also saying that the synoptic structure that I put together ten years ago still seems to be valid, or valid enough, and that I cannot see a case for pushing it any further. But maybe I lack the intellectual muscle and someone else will pick up where I left off.

The issues discussed above are represented visually in the pages that follow by means of a layout that separates the different putative authorial voices into separate columns. The reader should note that all the sentences (*pesukim*) are numbered sequentially in accordance with the standard text. By following the number at the start of each *pasuk*, it is possible to follow the Megillah in its conventional form, though this will not infrequently involve darting back and forth from one side of the page to the other. If, however, one reads down one or other of the two main columns one starts to hear with clarity the distinct tone of each of the two voices referred to above: the M voice (in the column adjacent to the gutter of the double page) and the E voice (in the outer column).

For convenience, the two columns have been separated by vertical rules. In a handful of cases the columns are further sub-divided. This is meant to show where additional information seems to have been interpolated, (a) to add extra detail or (b) to reinforce what had already been said (often resulting in unhelpful redundancy) or (c) out of editorial deference to the speaker, all presumably after the main text was established. More often than not, however, there is porosity between the columns where the story flips from one speaker to the other or where one speaker interjects with an alternative report. Where this is the case, the vertical rule is broken to allow the reader's gaze to slip sideways to discover the nature of the interruption. Towards the end of Chapter 9, however, the two voices are so insistently separate that the rule has been left unbroken. The reader must decide whether such a decision is warranted.

In general, passages that start on the same line but in different columns should be regarded as alternates and therefore equal in importance. Commentaries and amplifications that appear in sub-divided columns should be regarded as subsidiary or secondary to the main narrative thrust. Where the narrative is uncontested, it crosses the full page.

It is my hope that readers will find this edition of the *Megillah* helpful in opening up the full and until-now hidden richness of what the traditional text contains, as well as revealing self-evident duplications, redundancies and narrative contradictions. A key to the most telling divergences appears in the Notes at the end of the book.

Among those who have kindly given me the benefit of their advice and feedback during the writing of this study, I wish to thank Aaron J. Koller, Willem Smelik, Stephen Massil and Robin

Stamler for the always enjoyable correspondence that we have exchanged while the work was in preparation, and Raphaël Freeman and Zaki Elia for their thoughts on my typography. I also wish to thank Paul Shaviv for his generous endorsement, and my wife, Bracha (Bea) Games née Nemeth for first stoking my interest in the *Megillah*, following her own lead in learning the trope.

Stephen Games
Muswell Hill
2015–2026

The Synoptic Megillah

הַמְּגִלָּה הַסִינוֹפְּטִית

Megillat Esther
Chapter 1

Mordecai text (M)	Esther text (E)

1 Now it came to pass in the days of Ahasuerus

    (this is Ahasuerus who reigned from India to Ethiopia over a hundred and twenty-seven provinces)

2 In those days when King Ahasuerus sat on the throne of his kingdom

    (which was in Shushan fortress)

3 in the third year of his reign, he made a party for

all his princes and his servants,	the army of Persia and Media,	the nobles and princes of the provinces

being before him,

4 and he displayed the riches of his glorious kingdom and the honour of his excellent majesty for many days—even a hundred and eighty days. **5** And when these days were fulfilled,

the king made for all the people, great and small, that were in Shushan fortress a seven-day party in the court of the garden of the king's quarters. **6** There were hangings of white green and blue bordered by cords of linen and purple wool on rods of silver and pillars of marble. The couches were of gold and silver on a paved floor of green and white and shell and onyx marble. **7** Drinks were served in cups of gold, the cups being of various designs, with royal wine aplenty by the king's bounty.

8 And the drinking was according to the law: no one was forced to drink, for the king had ordered all the servants of his house that they should do only what it pleased them to do. [S]

9 Vashti the queen also made a party for the women in the royal house of King Ahasuerus.

10 On the seventh day

[W]hen the heart of the king was merry with wine he commanded Mehuman, Bizzetha, Harvona, Bigtha and Abagtha, Zethar and Carcas, the seven chamberlains that officiated in the presence of Ahasuerus the king, **11** to bring Queen Vashti before the king

wearing the royal crown

to show the peoples and the princes her beauty, for she was fair to look on.

12 But Queen Vashti refused to come at the king's commandment that the chamberlains had handed her, so the king was furious and his anger burned in him. [S]

13 Then the king said to the wise men who knew astrology

מְגִילַת אֶסְתֵּר
פֶּרֶק א

ESTHER TEXT (E)	MORDECAI TEXT (M)

MORDECAI TEXT (M)

1 וַיְהִי בִּימֵי אֲחַשְׁוֵרוֹשׁ

הוּא אֲחַשְׁוֵרוֹשׁ הַמֹּלֵךְ מֵהֹדּוּ וְעַד־כּוּשׁ שֶׁבַע וְעֶשְׂרִים וּמֵאָה מְדִינָה.

3 בִּשְׁנַת שָׁלוֹשׁ לְמָלְכוּ עָשָׂה מִשְׁתֶּה לְ-

כָּל־שָׂרָיו וַעֲבָדָיו	חֵיל פָּרַס וּמָדַי	הַפַּרְתְּמִים וְשָׂרֵי הַמְּדִינוֹת

לְפָנָיו.

4 בְּהַרְאֹתוֹ אֶת־עֹשֶׁר כְּבוֹד מַלְכוּתוֹ וְאֶת־יְקָר תִּפְאֶרֶת גְּדוּלָתוֹ יָמִים רַבִּים שְׁמוֹנִים וּמְאַת יוֹם. 5 וּבִמְלוֹאת הַיָּמִים הָאֵלֶּה

9 גַּם וַשְׁתִּי הַמַּלְכָּה עָשְׂתָה מִשְׁתֵּה נָשִׁים בֵּית הַמַּלְכוּת אֲשֶׁר לַמֶּלֶךְ אֲחַשְׁוֵרוֹשׁ.

בְּכֶתֶר מַלְכוּת

לְהַרְאוֹת הָעַמִּים וְהַשָּׂרִים אֶת־יָפְיָהּ כִּי־טוֹבַת מַרְאֶה הִיא.

ESTHER TEXT (E)

2 בַּיָּמִים הָהֵם כְּשֶׁבֶת הַמֶּלֶךְ אֲחַשְׁוֵרוֹשׁ עַל כִּסֵּא מַלְכוּתוֹ

אֲשֶׁר בְּשׁוּשַׁן הַבִּירָה.

עָשָׂה הַמֶּלֶךְ לְכָל־הָעָם הַנִּמְצָאִים בְּשׁוּשַׁן הַבִּירָה לְמִגָּדוֹל וְעַד־קָטָן מִשְׁתֶּה שִׁבְעַת יָמִים בַּחֲצַר גִּנַּת בִּיתַן הַמֶּלֶךְ. 6 חוּר כַּרְפַּס וּתְכֵלֶת אָחוּז בְּחַבְלֵי־בוּץ וְאַרְגָּמָן עַל־גְּלִילֵי כֶסֶף וְעַמּוּדֵי שֵׁשׁ מִטּוֹת זָהָב וָכֶסֶף עַל רִצְפַת בַּהַט־וָשֵׁשׁ וְדַר וְסֹחָרֶת. 7 וְהַשְׁקוֹת בִּכְלֵי זָהָב וְכֵלִים מִכֵּלִים שׁוֹנִים וְיֵין מַלְכוּת רָב כְּיַד הַמֶּלֶךְ. 8 וְהַשְּׁתִיָּה כַדָּת אֵין אֹנֵס כִּי־כֵן יִסַּד הַמֶּלֶךְ עַל כָּל־רַב בֵּיתוֹ לַעֲשׂוֹת כִּרְצוֹן אִישׁ־וָאִישׁ. [ס]

10 בַּיּוֹם הַשְּׁבִיעִי

כְּטוֹב לֵב־הַמֶּלֶךְ בַּיָּיִן אָמַר לִמְהוּמָן בִּזְּתָא חַרְבוֹנָא בִּגְתָא וַאֲבַגְתָא זֵתַר וְכַרְכַּס שִׁבְעַת הַסָּרִיסִים הַמְשָׁרְתִים אֶת־פְּנֵי הַמֶּלֶךְ אֲחַשְׁוֵרוֹשׁ. 11 לְהָבִיא אֶת־וַשְׁתִּי הַמַּלְכָּה לִפְנֵי הַמֶּלֶךְ

12 וַתְּמָאֵן הַמַּלְכָּה וַשְׁתִּי לָבוֹא בִּדְבַר הַמֶּלֶךְ אֲשֶׁר בְּיַד הַסָּרִיסִים וַיִּקְצֹף הַמֶּלֶךְ מְאֹד וַחֲמָתוֹ בָּעֲרָה בוֹ. [ס]

13 וַיֹּאמֶר הַמֶּלֶךְ לַחֲכָמִים יֹדְעֵי הָעִתִּים

15 'What by law can be done unto Queen Vashti since she has not carried out
the request of King Ahasuerus as sent by the chamberlains?' [S]

16 And Memucan answered before the king and the princes: 'Vashti the queen hath not done wrong
to the king only but also to all the princes and to all the peoples that are in all the provinces of the
king Ahasuerus. **17** For this deed of the queen will be revealed unto all women and make their
husbands contemptible in their eyes when it will be said: 'The King Ahasuerus commanded Vashti
the queen to be brought in before him but she came not.' **18** And this day will the princesses of
Persia and Media who have heard of the deed of the queen say the like unto all the king's princes.
So will there arise enough contempt and wrath. **19** If it please the king, let there go forth a royal
commandment from him and let it be written among the laws of the Persians and the Medes that
it be not altered that Vashti come no more before King Ahasuerus and that the king give her royal
estate unto another that is better than she. **20** And when the king's decree which he shall make shall
be published throughout all his kingdom, great though it be, all the wives will give to their husbands
honour both to great and small.' **21** And the word pleased the king and the princes, and the king
did according to the word of Memucan **22** for he sent letters

into all the king's provinces   into every province

*in its own script and to every people in their own language so that every man should
rule effectively in his own house by speaking in the language of his own people.* [S]

Chapter 2

1 After these things when the wrath of King Ahasuerus had subsided he remembered Vashti and what
she had done and what was decreed against her. **2** Then said the king's servants who ministered to him:
'Let there be sought for the king young virgins fair to look on **3** and let the king appoint officers in all
the provinces of his kingdom that they may gather together all the fair young virgins unto Shushan
fortress to the house of the women unto the custody of Hegai the king's chamberlain, keeper of the
women, and let their ointments be given them **4** and let the maiden that pleaseth the king be queen
instead of Vashti.' And the thing pleased the king and he did so. [S]

5 **There was a certain Jew in Shushan fortress whose name was Mordecai, the son of Jair,
the son of Shimei, the son of Kish, a Benjamite**

כִּי־כֵן דְּבַר הַמֶּלֶךְ לִפְנֵי
כָּל־יֹדְעֵי דָּת וָדִין.

14 וְהַקָּרֹב אֵלָיו
כַּרְשְׁנָא שֵׁתָר אַדְמָתָא
תַרְשִׁישׁ מֶרֶס מַרְסְנָא
מְמוּכָן שִׁבְעַת שָׂרֵי
פָּרַס וּמָדַי רֹאֵי פְּנֵי
הַמֶּלֶךְ הַיֹּשְׁבִים
רִאשֹׁנָה בַּמַּלְכוּת.

15 כְּדָת מַה־לַּעֲשׂוֹת בַּמַּלְכָּה וַשְׁתִּי עַל אֲשֶׁר לֹא־עָשְׂתָה
אֶת־מַאֲמַר הַמֶּלֶךְ אֲחַשְׁוֵרוֹשׁ בְּיַד הַסָּרִיסִים. [ס]

16 וַיֹּאמֶר מוּמְכָן (מְמוּכָן) לִפְנֵי הַמֶּלֶךְ וְהַשָּׂרִים לֹא עַל־הַמֶּלֶךְ לְבַדּוֹ עָוְתָה וַשְׁתִּי הַמַּלְכָּה
כִּי עַל־כָּל־הַשָּׂרִים וְעַל־כָּל־הָעַמִּים אֲשֶׁר בְּכָל־מְדִינוֹת הַמֶּלֶךְ אֲחַשְׁוֵרוֹשׁ. **17** כִּי־יֵצֵא דְבַר־
הַמַּלְכָּה עַל־כָּל־הַנָּשִׁים לְהַבְזוֹת בַּעְלֵיהֶן בְּעֵינֵיהֶן: בְּאָמְרָם הַמֶּלֶךְ אֲחַשְׁוֵרוֹשׁ אָמַר לְהָבִיא אֶת־
וַשְׁתִּי הַמַּלְכָּה לְפָנָיו וְלֹא־בָאָה. **18** וְהַיּוֹם הַזֶּה תֹּאמַרְנָה שָׂרוֹת פָּרַס־וּמָדַי אֲשֶׁר שָׁמְעוּ אֶת־דְּבַר
הַמַּלְכָּה לְכֹל שָׂרֵי הַמֶּלֶךְ וּכְדַי בִּזָּיוֹן וָקָצֶף. **19** אִם־עַל־הַמֶּלֶךְ טוֹב יֵצֵא דְבַר־מַלְכוּת מִלְּפָנָיו
וְיִכָּתֵב בְּדָתֵי פָרַס־וּמָדַי וְלֹא יַעֲבוֹר אֲשֶׁר לֹא־תָבוֹא וַשְׁתִּי לִפְנֵי הַמֶּלֶךְ אֲחַשְׁוֵרוֹשׁ וּמַלְכוּתָהּ יִתֵּן
הַמֶּלֶךְ לִרְעוּתָהּ הַטּוֹבָה מִמֶּנָּה. **20** וְנִשְׁמַע פִּתְגָם הַמֶּלֶךְ אֲשֶׁר־יַעֲשֶׂה בְּכָל־מַלְכוּתוֹ כִּי רַבָּה הִיא
וְכָל־הַנָּשִׁים יִתְּנוּ יְקָר לְבַעְלֵיהֶן לְמִגָּדוֹל וְעַד־קָטָן. **21** וַיִּיטַב הַדָּבָר בְּעֵינֵי הַמֶּלֶךְ וְהַשָּׂרִים וַיַּעַשׂ
הַמֶּלֶךְ כִּדְבַר מְמוּכָן. **22** וַיִּשְׁלַח סְפָרִים

אֶל־כָּל־מְדִינוֹת הַמֶּלֶךְ   אֶל־מְדִינָה וּמְדִינָה

כִּכְתָבָהּ וְאֶל־עַם וָעָם כִּלְשׁוֹנוֹ לִהְיוֹת כָּל־אִישׁ שֹׂרֵר בְּבֵיתוֹ וּמְדַבֵּר כִּלְשׁוֹן עַמּוֹ. [ס]

פֶּרֶק ב

1 אַחַר הַדְּבָרִים הָאֵלֶּה כְּשֹׁךְ חֲמַת הַמֶּלֶךְ אֲחַשְׁוֵרוֹשׁ זָכַר אֶת־וַשְׁתִּי וְאֵת אֲשֶׁר־עָשָׂתָה וְאֵת אֲשֶׁר־
נִגְזַר עָלֶיהָ. **2** וַיֹּאמְרוּ נַעֲרֵי־הַמֶּלֶךְ מְשָׁרְתָיו יְבַקְשׁוּ לַמֶּלֶךְ נְעָרוֹת בְּתוּלוֹת טוֹבוֹת מַרְאֶה. **3** וְיַפְקֵד
הַמֶּלֶךְ פְּקִידִים בְּכָל־מְדִינוֹת מַלְכוּתוֹ וְיִקְבְּצוּ אֶת־כָּל־נַעֲרָה־בְתוּלָה טוֹבַת מַרְאֶה אֶל־שׁוּשַׁן הַבִּירָה
אֶל־בֵּית הַנָּשִׁים אֶל־יַד הֵגֶא סְרִיס הַמֶּלֶךְ שֹׁמֵר הַנָּשִׁים וְנָתוֹן תַּמְרֻקֵיהֶן. **4** וְהַנַּעֲרָה אֲשֶׁר תִּיטַב
בְּעֵינֵי הַמֶּלֶךְ תִּמְלֹךְ תַּחַת וַשְׁתִּי וַיִּיטַב הַדָּבָר בְּעֵינֵי הַמֶּלֶךְ וַיַּעַשׂ כֵּן. [ס]

5 אִישׁ יְהוּדִי הָיָה בְּשׁוּשַׁן הַבִּירָה וּשְׁמוֹ מָרְדֳּכַי בֶּן יָאִיר בֶּן־שִׁמְעִי בֶּן־קִישׁ אִישׁ יְמִינִי.

6 who had been carried away from Jerusalem with the captives that were carried away with Jeconiah king of Judah whom Nebuchadnezzar the king of Babylon had carried away. **7** And he brought up

Hadassah	Esther
(his uncle's daughter,)	for she had neither father nor mother

and the maiden was of beautiful form and fair to look on

and when her father and mother were dead
Mordecai adopted her as his own daughter.

8 And so it was when the king's word and his decree were published and when many maidens were gathered together unto Shushan fortress (to the custody of Hegai) that Esther was taken

into the king's house	(to the custody of Hegai, keeper of the women)

9 and the maiden pleased him [*i.e. Ahasuerus*]   [*i.e. Hegai*]

and she obtained kindness of him.

and he speedily gave her her ointments with her portions and the seven maidens who were due to be given her out of the king's house, and he advanced her and her maidens to the best place in the house of the women.

(**10** Esther did not reveal her people or her kindred, for Mordecai had charged her that she should not tell it.)

(**11** And Mordecai walked every day before the court of the women's house to know how Esther did and what would become of her.)

12 Now when the turn of every maiden came to go in to King Ahasuerus, after that it had been done to her according to the law for the women twelve months (for thus were the days of their anointing carried out: six months with myrrh oil and six months with sweet odours and other feminine ointments), **13** then when a maiden came unto the king, whatsoever she desired was given her to go with her out of the house of the women unto the king's house. **14** In the evening she would go and next morning would return to the second house of the women, to the custody of Shaashgaz, the king's chamberlain who kept the concubines, and she would not return to the king unless the

6 אֲשֶׁר הָגְלָה מִירוּשָׁלַיִם עִם־הַגֹּלָה אֲשֶׁר הָגְלְתָה עִם יְכָנְיָה מֶלֶךְ־יְהוּדָה אֲשֶׁר הֶגְלָה נְבוּכַדְנֶצַּר מֶלֶךְ בָּבֶל. **7** וַיְהִי אֹמֵן

אֶת־הֲדַסָּה | הִיא אֶסְתֵּר

בַּת־דֹּדוֹ | כִּי אֵין לָהּ אָב וָאֵם

וְהַנַּעֲרָה יְפַת־תֹּאַר וְטוֹבַת מַרְאֶה

וּבְמוֹת אָבִיהָ וְאִמָּהּ לְקָחָהּ מָרְדֳּכַי לוֹ לְבַת.

8 וַיְהִי בְּהִשָּׁמַע דְּבַר־הַמֶּלֶךְ וְדָתוֹ וּבְהִקָּבֵץ נְעָרוֹת רַבּוֹת אֶל־שׁוּשַׁן הַבִּירָה אֶל־יַד הֵגַי וַתִּלָּקַח אֶסְתֵּר

אֶל־בֵּית הַמֶּלֶךְ | אֶל־יַד הֵגַי שֹׁמֵר הַנָּשִׁים.

9 וַתִּיטַב הַנַּעֲרָה בְעֵינָיו

וַתִּשָּׂא חֶסֶד לְפָנָיו | וַיְבַהֵל אֶת־תַּמְרוּקֶיהָ וְאֶת־מָנוֹתֶהָ לָתֵת לָהּ וְאֵת שֶׁבַע הַנְּעָרוֹת הָרְאֻיוֹת לָתֶת־לָהּ מִבֵּית הַמֶּלֶךְ וַיְשַׁנֶּהָ וְאֶת־נַעֲרוֹתֶיהָ לְטוֹב בֵּית הַנָּשִׁים.

10 לֹא־הִגִּידָה אֶסְתֵּר אֶת־עַמָּהּ וְאֶת־מוֹלַדְתָּהּ כִּי מָרְדֳּכַי צִוָּה עָלֶיהָ אֲשֶׁר לֹא־תַגִּיד.

11 וּבְכָל־יוֹם וָיוֹם מָרְדֳּכַי מִתְהַלֵּךְ לִפְנֵי חֲצַר בֵּית־הַנָּשִׁים לָדַעַת אֶת־שְׁלוֹם אֶסְתֵּר וּמַה־יֵּעָשֶׂה בָּהּ.

12 וּבְהַגִּיעַ תֹּר נַעֲרָה וְנַעֲרָה לָבוֹא אֶל־הַמֶּלֶךְ אֲחַשְׁוֵרוֹשׁ מִקֵּץ הֱיוֹת לָהּ כְּדָת הַנָּשִׁים שְׁנֵים עָשָׂר חֹדֶשׁ כִּי כֵּן יִמְלְאוּ יְמֵי מְרוּקֵיהֶן שִׁשָּׁה חֳדָשִׁים בְּשֶׁמֶן הַמֹּר וְשִׁשָּׁה חֳדָשִׁים בַּבְּשָׂמִים וּבְתַמְרוּקֵי הַנָּשִׁים. **13** וּבָזֶה הַנַּעֲרָה בָּאָה אֶל־הַמֶּלֶךְ אֵת כָּל־אֲשֶׁר תֹּאמַר יִנָּתֵן לָהּ לָבוֹא עִמָּהּ מִבֵּית הַנָּשִׁים עַד־בֵּית הַמֶּלֶךְ. **14** בָּעֶרֶב הִיא בָאָה וּבַבֹּקֶר הִיא שָׁבָה אֶל־בֵּית הַנָּשִׁים שֵׁנִי אֶל־יַד שַׁעַשְׁגַז סְרִיס הַמֶּלֶךְ שֹׁמֵר הַפִּילַגְשִׁים לֹא־תָבוֹא עוֹד אֶל־הַמֶּלֶךְ כִּי אִם־חָפֵץ בָּהּ

king delighted in her and she was called for by name.) **15** Now when came the turn of Esther

(the daughter of Abihail,

> (the uncle of Mordecai who took her as his daughter)

to go to the king, she only needed what Hegai the king's chamberlain, keeper of the women, decided.

(Everyone who saw Esther adored her.)

16 So Esther was taken unto King Ahasuerus into his house royal in the tenth month

(which is the month of Tevet)　(in the seventh year of his reign).

17 And the king loved Esther above all the women and she obtained grace and favour in his sight more than all the virgins so that he set the royal crown upon her head and made her queen instead of Vashti. **18** Then the king made a great feast unto all his princes and his servants, even Esther's feast, and he made a release to the provinces and gave gifts according to the bounty of the king.

19 (And the virgins were gathered again . . .)

(And Mordecai sat in the king's gate . . .)

20 Esther had not yet revealed who her kindred were, nor her people, as Mordecai had told her, for Esther did what Mordecai instructed her, just as she had when she was brought up by him. [S]

21 In those days, while Mordecai sat in the king's gate, Bigthan and Teresh, two of the king's chamberlains that guarded the door, were wroth and sought to lay hands on the king Ahasuerus. **22** And the thing became known to Mordecai who told it unto Queen Esther, and Esther told the king thereof in Mordecai's name. **23** And when inquisition was made of the matter and it was found to be so, they were both hanged on a tree and it was written in the *Book of Chronicles* before the king. [S]

Chapter 3

1 After these events King Ahasuerus promoted **Haman** the son of Hammedatha the Agagite and advanced him and set his seat above all the princes that were with him.

הַמֶּלֶךְ וְנִקְרְאָה בְשֵׁם. **15** וּבְהַגִּיעַ תֹּר־אֶסְתֵּר
בַת־אֲבִיחַיִל

דֹּד מָרְדֳּכַי אֲשֶׁר
לָקַח־לוֹ לְבַת

לָבוֹא אֶל־הַמֶּלֶךְ לֹא בִקְשָׁה דָּבָר כִּי אִם אֶת־
אֲשֶׁר יֹאמַר הֵגַי סְרִיס־הַמֶּלֶךְ שֹׁמֵר הַנָּשִׁים

וַתְּהִי אֶסְתֵּר נֹשֵׂאת חֵן בְּעֵינֵי כָּל־רֹאֶיהָ.

16 וַתִּלָּקַח אֶסְתֵּר אֶל־הַמֶּלֶךְ אֲחַשְׁוֵרוֹשׁ אֶל־
בֵּית מַלְכוּתוֹ בַּחֹדֶשׁ הָעֲשִׂירִי

בִּשְׁנַת־שֶׁבַע לְמַלְכוּתוֹ. | הוּא־חֹדֶשׁ טֵבֵת

17 וַיֶּאֱהַב הַמֶּלֶךְ אֶת־אֶסְתֵּר מִכָּל־הַנָּשִׁים וַתִּשָּׂא־חֵן וָחֶסֶד לְפָנָיו מִכָּל־הַבְּתוּלוֹת
וַיָּשֶׂם כֶּתֶר־מַלְכוּת בְּרֹאשָׁהּ וַיַּמְלִיכֶהָ תַּחַת וַשְׁתִּי. **18** וַיַּעַשׂ הַמֶּלֶךְ מִשְׁתֶּה
גָדוֹל לְכָל־שָׂרָיו וַעֲבָדָיו אֵת מִשְׁתֵּה אֶסְתֵּר וַהֲנָחָה לַמְּדִינוֹת עָשָׂה וַיִּתֵּן
מַשְׂאֵת כְּיַד הַמֶּלֶךְ.

19 וּבְהִקָּבֵץ
בְּתוּלוֹת שֵׁנִית

וּמָרְדֳּכַי יֹשֵׁב בְּשַׁעַר־
הַמֶּלֶךְ.

20 אֵין אֶסְתֵּר מַגֶּדֶת מוֹלַדְתָּהּ וְאֶת־עַמָּהּ כַּאֲשֶׁר
צִוָּה עָלֶיהָ מָרְדֳּכָי וְאֶת־מַאֲמַר מָרְדֳּכַי אֶסְתֵּר
עֹשָׂה כַּאֲשֶׁר הָיְתָה בְאָמְנָה אִתּוֹ. [ס]

21 בַּיָּמִים הָהֵם וּמָרְדֳּכַי יוֹשֵׁב בְּשַׁעַר־הַמֶּלֶךְ קָצַף בִּגְתָן וָתֶרֶשׁ שְׁנֵי־סָרִיסֵי הַמֶּלֶךְ מִשֹּׁמְרֵי
הַסַּף וַיְבַקְשׁוּ לִשְׁלֹחַ יָד בַּמֶּלֶךְ אֲחַשְׁוֵרֹשׁ. **22** וַיִּוָּדַע הַדָּבָר לְמָרְדֳּכַי וַיַּגֵּד לְאֶסְתֵּר הַמַּלְכָּה
וַתֹּאמֶר אֶסְתֵּר לַמֶּלֶךְ בְּשֵׁם מָרְדֳּכָי. **23** וַיְבֻקַּשׁ הַדָּבָר וַיִּמָּצֵא וַיִּתָּלוּ שְׁנֵיהֶם עַל־עֵץ וַיִּכָּתֵב
בְּסֵפֶר דִּבְרֵי הַיָּמִים לִפְנֵי הַמֶּלֶךְ. [ס]

פֶּרֶק ג

1 אַחַר הַדְּבָרִים הָאֵלֶּה גִּדַּל הַמֶּלֶךְ אֲחַשְׁוֵרוֹשׁ אֶת־הָמָן בֶּן־הַמְּדָתָא הָאֲגָגִי וַיְנַשְּׂאֵהוּ וַיָּשֶׂם
אֶת־כִּסְאוֹ מֵעַל כָּל־הַשָּׂרִים אֲשֶׁר אִתּוֹ.

2 And all the king's servants that were in the king's gate bowed down and prostrated themselves before **Haman** for the king had so commanded concerning him. But Mordecai neither bowed down nor prostrated himself before him. **3** Then the king's servants that were in the king's gate said unto Mordecai: 'Why do you transgress the king's commandment?' **4** Now it came to pass that they spoke daily unto him and he hearkened not unto them, so they told **Haman** to see whether Mordecai's words would be allowed to stand, for he had told them that he was a Jew. **5** When **Haman** saw that Mordecai neither bowed down nor prostrated himself before him then was **Haman** full of wrath. **6** But it seemed contemptible in his eyes to lay hands on Mordecai alone, for they had made known to him the people of Mordecai, so **Haman** sought to destroy all the Jews throughout the whole kingdom of Ahasuerus—the people of Mordecai.

7 In the first month (i.e, the month of Niysan) (in the twelfth year of [the reign of] King Ahasuerus) they cast *pur* (i.e. the *lot*) before **Haman** [to determine] the day and the month [until it fell on] the twelfth month (which is the month of Adar). [S]

8 And **Haman** said unto King Ahasuerus: 'There is a certain people scattered abroad and dispersed among the peoples in all the provinces of thy kingdom and their laws are diverse from those of every people, neither keep they the king's laws, therefore it profiteth not the king to suffer them. **9** If it please the king let it be written that they be destroyed and I will pay ten thousand talents of silver into the hands of those that have the charge of the king's business to bring it into the king's treasuries.' **10** And the king took his ring from his hand and gave it unto **Haman** the son of Hammedatha the Agagite, the Jews' enemy. **11** And the king said

2 וְכָל־עַבְדֵי הַמֶּלֶךְ אֲשֶׁר־בְּשַׁעַר הַמֶּלֶךְ כֹּרְעִים וּמִשְׁתַּחֲוִים לְהָמָן כִּי־כֵן צִוָּה־לוֹ הַמֶּלֶךְ וּמָרְדֳּכַי לֹא יִכְרַע וְלֹא יִשְׁתַּחֲוֶה. **3** וַיֹּאמְרוּ עַבְדֵי הַמֶּלֶךְ אֲשֶׁר־בְּשַׁעַר הַמֶּלֶךְ לְמָרְדֳּכָי מַדּוּעַ אַתָּה עוֹבֵר אֵת מִצְוַת הַמֶּלֶךְ. **4** וַיְהִי באמרם (כְּאָמְרָם) אֵלָיו יוֹם וָיוֹם וְלֹא שָׁמַע אֲלֵיהֶם וַיַּגִּידוּ לְהָמָן לִרְאוֹת הֲיַעַמְדוּ דִּבְרֵי מָרְדֳּכַי כִּי־הִגִּיד לָהֶם אֲשֶׁר־הוּא יְהוּדִי. **5** וַיַּרְא הָמָן כִּי־אֵין מָרְדֳּכַי כֹּרֵעַ וּמִשְׁתַּחֲוֶה לוֹ וַיִּמָּלֵא הָמָן חֵמָה. **6** וַיִּבֶז בְּעֵינָיו לִשְׁלֹחַ יָד בְּמָרְדֳּכַי לְבַדּוֹ כִּי־הִגִּידוּ לוֹ אֶת־עַם מָרְדֳּכָי וַיְבַקֵּשׁ הָמָן לְהַשְׁמִיד אֶת־כָּל־הַיְּהוּדִים אֲשֶׁר בְּכָל־מַלְכוּת אֲחַשְׁוֵרוֹשׁ עַם מָרְדֳּכָי.

7 בַּחֹדֶשׁ הָרִאשׁוֹן הוּא־חֹדֶשׁ נִיסָן בִּשְׁנַת שְׁתֵּים עֶשְׂרֵה לַמֶּלֶךְ אֲחַשְׁוֵרוֹשׁ הִפִּיל פּוּר הוּא הַגּוֹרָל לִפְנֵי הָמָן מִיּוֹם לְיוֹם וּמֵחֹדֶשׁ לְחֹדֶשׁ שְׁנֵים־עָשָׂר הוּא־חֹדֶשׁ אֲדָר. [ס]

8 וַיֹּאמֶר הָמָן לַמֶּלֶךְ אֲחַשְׁוֵרוֹשׁ יֶשְׁנוֹ עַם־אֶחָד מְפֻזָּר וּמְפֹרָד בֵּין הָעַמִּים בְּכֹל מְדִינוֹת מַלְכוּתֶךָ וְדָתֵיהֶם שֹׁנוֹת מִכָּל־עָם וְאֶת־דָּתֵי הַמֶּלֶךְ אֵינָם עֹשִׂים וְלַמֶּלֶךְ אֵין־שֹׁוֶה לְהַנִּיחָם. **9** אִם־עַל־הַמֶּלֶךְ טוֹב יִכָּתֵב לְאַבְּדָם וַעֲשֶׂרֶת אֲלָפִים כִּכַּר־כֶּסֶף אֶשְׁקוֹל עַל־יְדֵי עֹשֵׂי הַמְּלָאכָה לְהָבִיא אֶל־גִּנְזֵי הַמֶּלֶךְ. **10** וַיָּסַר הַמֶּלֶךְ אֶת־טַבַּעְתּוֹ מֵעַל יָדוֹ וַיִּתְּנָהּ לְהָמָן בֶּן־הַמְּדָתָא הָאֲגָגִי צֹרֵר הַיְּהוּדִים. **11** וַיֹּאמֶר הַמֶּלֶךְ

unto **Haman**: 'The silver is given to you; the people also are yours to do with as you like.'

12 Then were the king's scribes called in the first month on the thirteenth day thereof and there was written according to all that **Haman** commanded

to the king's satraps and to the governors that were over every province and to the princes of every people;

to every province according to the writing thereof, and to every people after their language;

in the name of king Ahasuerus was it written and it was sealed with the king's ring.

13 And documents were sent by posts into all the king's provinces to destroy, to slay and to cause to perish all Jews, young and old, little children and women, in one day even, upon the thirteenth day of the twelfth month which is the month Adar and to take the spoil of them for a prey.

14 The copy of the text for release as a decree in every province was to be published for all peoples so they should be ready against that day.

15 The posts went forth in haste by the king's commandment and the decree was given out in Shushan castle.

And the king and **Haman** sat down to drink but the city of Shushan was troubled. [S]

Chapter 4

1 Now when Mordecai knew all that was done Mordecai rent his clothes and put on sackcloth and ashes and went out into the midst of the city and cried with a loud and a bitter cry. **2** And he came even as far as the king's gate (for none might enter within the king's gate clothed in sackcloth).

3 In every province wherever the king's law and his decree came there was great mourning among the Jews and fasting and weeping and wailing, and many lay in sackcloth and ashes.

4 And Esther's maidens and her chamberlains came and told this to her and the queen was much pained and sent raiment to clothe Mordecai and to take his sackcloth from him but he accepted it not.

5 And Esther called for Hathach, one of the king's chamberlains whom he had appointed to attend upon her, and charged him to go to Mordecai to know what this was and why it was.

6 So Hathach went forth to Mordecai unto the main street of the city which was before the king's gate.

לְהָמָן הַכֶּסֶף נָתוּן לָךְ וְהָעָם לַעֲשׂוֹת בּוֹ כַּטּוֹב בְּעֵינֶיךָ.

12 וַיִּקָּרְאוּ סֹפְרֵי הַמֶּלֶךְ בַּחֹדֶשׁ הָרִאשׁוֹן בִּשְׁלוֹשָׁה עָשָׂר יוֹם בּוֹ וַיִּכָּתֵב כְּכָל־אֲשֶׁר־צִוָּה הָמָן אֶל

אֲחַשְׁדַּרְפְּנֵי־הַמֶּלֶךְ מְדִינָה וּמְדִינָה
וְאֶל־הַפַּחוֹת אֲשֶׁר כִּכְתָבָהּ וְעַם וָעָם
עַל־מְדִינָה וּמְדִינָה כִּלְשׁוֹנוֹ:
וְאֶל־שָׂרֵי עַם וָעָם:

בְּשֵׁם הַמֶּלֶךְ אֲחַשְׁוֵרֹשׁ נִכְתָּב וְנֶחְתָּם בְּטַבַּעַת הַמֶּלֶךְ

13 וְנִשְׁלוֹחַ סְפָרִים בְּיַד הָרָצִים אֶל־כָּל־מְדִינוֹת הַמֶּלֶךְ לְהַשְׁמִיד לַהֲרֹג וּלְאַבֵּד אֶת־כָּל־הַיְּהוּדִים מִנַּעַר וְעַד־זָקֵן טַף וְנָשִׁים בְּיוֹם אֶחָד בִּשְׁלוֹשָׁה עָשָׂר לְחֹדֶשׁ שְׁנֵים־עָשָׂר הוּא־חֹדֶשׁ אֲדָר וּשְׁלָלָם לָבוֹז.

14 פַּתְשֶׁגֶן הַכְּתָב לְהִנָּתֵן דָּת בְּכָל־מְדִינָה וּמְדִינָה גָּלוּי לְכָל־הָעַמִּים לִהְיוֹת עֲתִדִים לַיּוֹם הַזֶּה.

15 הָרָצִים יָצְאוּ דְחוּפִים בִּדְבַר הַמֶּלֶךְ וְהַדָּת נִתְּנָה בְּשׁוּשַׁן הַבִּירָה

וְהַמֶּלֶךְ וְהָמָן יָשְׁבוּ לִשְׁתּוֹת וְהָעִיר שׁוּשָׁן נָבוֹכָה. [ס]

פֶּרֶק ד

1 וּמָרְדֳּכַי יָדַע אֶת־כָּל־אֲשֶׁר נַעֲשָׂה וַיִּקְרַע מָרְדֳּכַי אֶת־בְּגָדָיו וַיִּלְבַּשׁ שַׂק וָאֵפֶר וַיֵּצֵא בְּתוֹךְ הָעִיר וַיִּזְעַק זְעָקָה גְדוֹלָה וּמָרָה. **2** וַיָּבוֹא עַד לִפְנֵי שַׁעַר־הַמֶּלֶךְ כִּי אֵין לָבוֹא אֶל־שַׁעַר הַמֶּלֶךְ בִּלְבוּשׁ שָׂק.

3 וּבְכָל־מְדִינָה וּמְדִינָה מְקוֹם אֲשֶׁר דְּבַר־הַמֶּלֶךְ וְדָתוֹ מַגִּיעַ אֵבֶל גָּדוֹל לַיְּהוּדִים וְצוֹם וּבְכִי וּמִסְפֵּד שַׂק וָאֵפֶר יֻצַּע לָרַבִּים.

4 וַתָּבוֹאינָה (וַתָּבוֹאנָה) נַעֲרוֹת אֶסְתֵּר וְסָרִיסֶיהָ וַיַּגִּידוּ לָהּ וַתִּתְחַלְחַל הַמַּלְכָּה מְאֹד וַתִּשְׁלַח בְּגָדִים לְהַלְבִּישׁ אֶת־מָרְדֳּכַי וּלְהָסִיר שַׂקּוֹ מֵעָלָיו וְלֹא קִבֵּל.

5 וַתִּקְרָא אֶסְתֵּר לַהֲתָךְ מִסָּרִיסֵי הַמֶּלֶךְ אֲשֶׁר הֶעֱמִיד לְפָנֶיהָ וַתְּצַוֵּהוּ עַל־מָרְדֳּכָי לָדַעַת מַה־זֶּה וְעַל־מַה־זֶּה.

6 וַיֵּצֵא הֲתָךְ אֶל־מָרְדֳּכָי אֶל־רְחוֹב הָעִיר אֲשֶׁר לִפְנֵי שַׁעַר־הַמֶּלֶךְ.

7 And Mordecai told him all that had happened unto him and the exact sum of the money that **Haman** had promised to pay into the king's treasuries for the Jews to destroy them. **8** Also he gave him the copy of the writing of the decree that was given out in Shushan to destroy them to show it unto Esther and to declare it unto her and charge her that she should go in unto the king to make supplication unto him and to entreat before him for her people. **9** And Hathach came and told Esther the words of Mordecai. **10** Then Esther spoke unto Hathach and gave him a message for Mordecai: **11** 'All the king's servants and the people of the king's provinces do know that every man or woman who shall come unto the king into the inner court who is not called, there is one law for him: that he be put to death, except to whom the king shall hold out the golden sceptre that he may live, and I have not been called to come in unto the king these thirty days.' **12** And they told Mordecai Esther's words. **13** Then Mordecai bade them to reply unto Esther: 'Think not with thyself that thou shalt escape in the king's house more than all the Jews. **14** For if thou altogether holdest thy peace at this time then will relief and deliverance arise to the Jews from another place but thou and thy father's house will perish; and who knoweth whether thou art not come to royal estate for such a time as this?' **15** Then Esther bade them return answer unto Mordecai: **16** 'Go gather together all the Jews that are present in Shushan and fast ye for me and neither eat nor drink three days night or day; I also and my maidens will fast in like manner; and so will I go in unto the king which is not according to the law; and if I perish I perish.' **17** So Mordecai went his way and did according to all that Esther had commanded him.

Chapter 5

1 Now it came to pass on the third day that Esther put on her royal apparel and stood in the inner court of the king's house in sight of the king's house and the king sat upon his royal throne in the royal house in sight of the entrance of the house. **2** And it was so when the king saw Esther the queen standing in the court that she obtained favour in his sight and the king held out to Esther the golden sceptre that was in his hand. So Esther drew near and touched the top of the sceptre. **3** Then said the king unto her: 'What wilt thou, Queen Esther? for whatever thy request even to the half of the kingdom it shall be given thee.'

4 And Esther said: 'If it please the king let the king and **Haman** come this day unto the party that I have prepared for him.' **5** Then the king said: 'Cause **Haman** to hurry so it may be done as Esther hath said.' So the king and **Haman** came to the party that Esther had prepared.

6 And the king said to Esther at the party of wine: 'Whatever thy petition it shall be granted thee and whatever thy request even to the half of the kingdom it shall be performed.'

7 Then answered Esther and said: 'My petition and my request is that **8** if I have found favour in the sight of the king and if it please the king to grant my petition and to perform my request let the king and **Haman** come to the party that I shall prepare for them and I will do tomorrow as the king hath said.' **9** Then went **Haman** forth that day full of joy and glad of heart but when **Haman** saw that Mordecai in the king's gate neither stood up nor moved for him, **Haman** was filled with wrath against Mordecai. **10** **Haman** nevertheless refrained himself and went home and sent and fetched his friends and Zeresh his wife. **11** And **Haman** recounted unto them the glory of his riches and the multitude of his children and everything as to how the king had promoted him and how he had advanced him above the princes and servants of the king. **12** **Haman** said moreover: 'Yea Esther the queen did let no man come in with the king unto the party that she had prepared but myself; and tomorrow also am I invited by her together with the king. **13** Yet all this availeth me nothing so long as I see Mordecai the Jew sitting at the king's gate.' **14** Then said Zeresh his wife and all his friends unto him: 'Let a gallows be made of fifty cubits high and in the morning speak thou unto the king that Mordecai may be hanged thereon; then go thou in merrily with the king unto the banquet.' And the thing pleased **Haman** and he caused the gallows to be made. [S]

7 וַיַּגֶּד־לוֹ מָרְדֳּכַי אֵת כָּל־אֲשֶׁר קָרָהוּ וְאֵת פָּרָשַׁת הַכֶּסֶף אֲשֶׁר אָמַר הָמָן לִשְׁקוֹל עַל־גִּנְזֵי הַמֶּלֶךְ בַּיְּהוּדִיִּים (בַּיְּהוּדִים) לְאַבְּדָם. **8** וְאֶת־פַּתְשֶׁגֶן כְּתָב־הַדָּת אֲשֶׁר־נִתַּן בְּשׁוּשָׁן לְהַשְׁמִידָם נָתַן לוֹ לְהַרְאוֹת אֶת־אֶסְתֵּר וּלְהַגִּיד לָהּ וּלְצַוּוֹת עָלֶיהָ לָבוֹא אֶל־הַמֶּלֶךְ לְהִתְחַנֶּן־לוֹ וּלְבַקֵּשׁ מִלְּפָנָיו עַל־עַמָּהּ. **9** וַיָּבוֹא הֲתָךְ וַיַּגֵּד לְאֶסְתֵּר אֵת דִּבְרֵי מָרְדֳּכָי. **10** וַתֹּאמֶר אֶסְתֵּר לַהֲתָךְ וַתְּצַוֵּהוּ אֶל־מָרְדֳּכָי.

11 כָּל־עַבְדֵי הַמֶּלֶךְ וְעַם־מְדִינוֹת הַמֶּלֶךְ יֹדְעִים אֲשֶׁר כָּל־אִישׁ וְאִשָּׁה אֲשֶׁר יָבוֹא־אֶל־הַמֶּלֶךְ אֶל־הֶחָצֵר הַפְּנִימִית אֲשֶׁר לֹא־יִקָּרֵא אַחַת דָּתוֹ לְהָמִית לְבַד מֵאֲשֶׁר יוֹשִׁיט־לוֹ הַמֶּלֶךְ אֶת־שַׁרְבִיט הַזָּהָב וְחָיָה וַאֲנִי לֹא נִקְרֵאתִי לָבוֹא אֶל־הַמֶּלֶךְ זֶה שְׁלוֹשִׁים יוֹם. **12** וַיַּגִּידוּ לְמָרְדֳּכָי אֵת דִּבְרֵי אֶסְתֵּר.

13 וַיֹּאמֶר מָרְדֳּכַי לְהָשִׁיב אֶל־אֶסְתֵּר אַל־תְּדַמִּי בְנַפְשֵׁךְ לְהִמָּלֵט בֵּית־הַמֶּלֶךְ מִכָּל־הַיְּהוּדִים.

14 כִּי אִם־הַחֲרֵשׁ תַּחֲרִישִׁי בָּעֵת הַזֹּאת רֶוַח וְהַצָּלָה יַעֲמוֹד לַיְּהוּדִים מִמָּקוֹם אַחֵר וְאַתְּ וּבֵית־אָבִיךְ תֹּאבֵדוּ וּמִי יוֹדֵעַ אִם־לְעֵת כָּזֹאת הִגַּעַתְּ לַמַּלְכוּת. **15** וַתֹּאמֶר אֶסְתֵּר לְהָשִׁיב אֶל־מָרְדֳּכָי. **16** לֵךְ כְּנוֹס אֶת־כָּל־הַיְּהוּדִים הַנִּמְצְאִים בְּשׁוּשָׁן וְצוּמוּ עָלַי וְאַל־תֹּאכְלוּ וְאַל־תִּשְׁתּוּ שְׁלֹשֶׁת יָמִים לַיְלָה וָיוֹם גַּם־אֲנִי וְנַעֲרֹתַי אָצוּם כֵּן וּבְכֵן אָבוֹא אֶל־הַמֶּלֶךְ אֲשֶׁר לֹא־כַדָּת וְכַאֲשֶׁר אָבַדְתִּי אָבָדְתִּי.

17 וַיַּעֲבֹר מָרְדֳּכָי וַיַּעַשׂ כְּכֹל אֲשֶׁר־צִוְּתָה עָלָיו אֶסְתֵּר.

פֶּרֶק ה

1 וַיְהִי בַּיּוֹם הַשְּׁלִישִׁי וַתִּלְבַּשׁ אֶסְתֵּר מַלְכוּת וַתַּעֲמֹד בַּחֲצַר בֵּית־הַמֶּלֶךְ הַפְּנִימִית נֹכַח בֵּית הַמֶּלֶךְ וְהַמֶּלֶךְ יוֹשֵׁב עַל־כִּסֵּא מַלְכוּתוֹ בְּבֵית הַמַּלְכוּת נֹכַח פֶּתַח הַבָּיִת. **2** וַיְהִי כִרְאוֹת הַמֶּלֶךְ אֶת־אֶסְתֵּר הַמַּלְכָּה עֹמֶדֶת בֶּחָצֵר נָשְׂאָה חֵן בְּעֵינָיו וַיּוֹשֶׁט הַמֶּלֶךְ לְאֶסְתֵּר אֶת־שַׁרְבִיט הַזָּהָב אֲשֶׁר בְּיָדוֹ וַתִּקְרַב אֶסְתֵּר וַתִּגַּע בְּרֹאשׁ הַשַּׁרְבִיט. **3** וַיֹּאמֶר לָהּ הַמֶּלֶךְ מַה־לָּךְ אֶסְתֵּר הַמַּלְכָּה וּמַה־בַּקָּשָׁתֵךְ עַד־חֲצִי הַמַּלְכוּת וְיִנָּתֵן לָךְ.

4 וַתֹּאמֶר אֶסְתֵּר אִם־עַל־הַמֶּלֶךְ טוֹב יָבוֹא הַמֶּלֶךְ וְהָמָן הַיּוֹם אֶל־הַמִּשְׁתֶּה אֲשֶׁר־עָשִׂיתִי לוֹ. **5** וַיֹּאמֶר הַמֶּלֶךְ מַהֲרוּ אֶת־הָמָן לַעֲשׂוֹת אֶת־דְּבַר אֶסְתֵּר וַיָּבֹא הַמֶּלֶךְ וְהָמָן אֶל־הַמִּשְׁתֶּה אֲשֶׁר־עָשְׂתָה אֶסְתֵּר. **6** וַיֹּאמֶר הַמֶּלֶךְ לְאֶסְתֵּר בְּמִשְׁתֵּה הַיַּיִן מַה־שְּׁאֵלָתֵךְ וְיִנָּתֵן לָךְ וּמַה־בַּקָּשָׁתֵךְ עַד־חֲצִי הַמַּלְכוּת וְתֵעָשׂ.

7 וַתַּעַן אֶסְתֵּר וַתֹּאמַר שְׁאֵלָתִי וּבַקָּשָׁתִי. **8** אִם־מָצָאתִי חֵן בְּעֵינֵי הַמֶּלֶךְ וְאִם־עַל־הַמֶּלֶךְ טוֹב לָתֵת אֶת־שְׁאֵלָתִי וְלַעֲשׂוֹת אֶת־בַּקָּשָׁתִי יָבוֹא הַמֶּלֶךְ וְהָמָן אֶל־הַמִּשְׁתֶּה אֲשֶׁר אֶעֱשֶׂה לָהֶם וּמָחָר אֶעֱשֶׂה כִּדְבַר הַמֶּלֶךְ.

9 וַיֵּצֵא הָמָן בַּיּוֹם הַהוּא שָׂמֵחַ וְטוֹב לֵב וְכִרְאוֹת הָמָן אֶת־מָרְדֳּכַי בְּשַׁעַר הַמֶּלֶךְ וְלֹא־קָם וְלֹא־זָע מִמֶּנּוּ וַיִּמָּלֵא הָמָן עַל־מָרְדֳּכַי חֵמָה.

10 וַיִּתְאַפַּק הָמָן וַיָּבוֹא אֶל־בֵּיתוֹ וַיִּשְׁלַח וַיָּבֵא אֶת־אֹהֲבָיו וְאֶת־זֶרֶשׁ אִשְׁתּוֹ. **11** וַיְסַפֵּר לָהֶם הָמָן אֶת־כְּבוֹד עָשְׁרוֹ וְרֹב בָּנָיו וְאֵת כָּל־אֲשֶׁר גִּדְּלוֹ הַמֶּלֶךְ וְאֵת אֲשֶׁר נִשְּׂאוֹ עַל־הַשָּׂרִים וְעַבְדֵי הַמֶּלֶךְ. **12** וַיֹּאמֶר הָמָן אַף לֹא־הֵבִיאָה אֶסְתֵּר הַמַּלְכָּה עִם־הַמֶּלֶךְ אֶל־הַמִּשְׁתֶּה אֲשֶׁר־עָשָׂתָה כִּי אִם־אוֹתִי וְגַם־לְמָחָר אֲנִי קָרוּא־לָהּ עִם־הַמֶּלֶךְ. **13** וְכָל־זֶה אֵינֶנּוּ שֹׁוֶה לִי בְּכָל־עֵת אֲשֶׁר אֲנִי רֹאֶה אֶת־מָרְדֳּכַי הַיְּהוּדִי יוֹשֵׁב בְּשַׁעַר הַמֶּלֶךְ. **14** וַתֹּאמֶר לוֹ זֶרֶשׁ אִשְׁתּוֹ וְכָל־אֹהֲבָיו יַעֲשׂוּ־עֵץ גָּבֹהַּ חֲמִשִּׁים אַמָּה וּבַבֹּקֶר אֱמֹר לַמֶּלֶךְ וְיִתְלוּ אֶת־מָרְדֳּכַי עָלָיו וּבֹא־עִם־הַמֶּלֶךְ אֶל־הַמִּשְׁתֶּה שָׂמֵחַ וַיִּיטַב הַדָּבָר לִפְנֵי הָמָן וַיַּעַשׂ הָעֵץ. [ס]

Chapter 6

1 On that night the king could not sleep and he commanded to bring the book of records of the *Book of Chronicles* and they were read before the king. **2** And it was found written that Mordecai had told of Bigthana and Teresh, two of the king's chamberlains of those that guarded the door, who had sought to lay hands on king Ahasuerus. **3** And the king said: 'What honour and dignity hath been done to Mordecai for this?' Then said the king's servants that ministered unto him: 'There is nothing done for him.' **4** And the king said: 'Who is in the court?'

—Now **Haman** came to the outer court of the king's house to speak unto the king to hang Mordecai on the gallows that he had prepared for him.—

5 And the king's servants said to him: 'Behold **Haman** standeth in the court.' And the king said: 'Let him come in.' **6** So **Haman** came in. And the king said to him: 'What shall be done to the man whom the king delighteth to honour?'

—Now **Haman** said in his heart: 'Whom would the king delight to honour besides myself?'—

7 And **Haman** said unto the king: 'For the man whom the king delighteth to honour **8** let be brought royal apparel that the king useth to wear and the horse that the king rideth upon and set a royal crown on his head **9** and let the apparel and the horse be delivered to the hand of one of the king's noblest princes so they may array therewith the man whom the king delighteth to honour and cause him to ride on horseback through the street of the city and proclaim before him: "Thus shall it be done to the man whom the king delighteth to honour."' **10** Then the king said to **Haman**: 'Hurry and take the apparel and the horse as thou hast said and do even so to Mordecai the Jew that sitteth at the king's gate. Let nothing fail of all that thou hast spoken.' **11** Then **Haman** took the apparel and the horse and arrayed Mordecai and caused him to ride through the street[s] of the city and proclaimed before him: 'Thus shall it be done unto the man whom the king delighteth to honour.' **12** And Mordecai returned to the king's gate but **Haman** hurried home, mourning and with his head covered. **13** And **Haman** told Zeresh his wife and all his friends all that had happened. Then said his wise men and Zeresh his wife unto him: 'If Mordecai before whom thou hast begun to fall be of the seed of the Jews thou shalt not prevail against him but shalt surely fall before him.' **14** While they were yet talking with him the king's eunuchs came and hastened to bring **Haman** unto the party that Esther had prepared.

Chapter 7

1 So the king and **Haman** came to party with Esther the queen. **2** And the king said again unto Esther on the second day at the party of wine: 'Whatever thy petition Queen Esther it shall be granted thee and whatever thy request even to the half of the kingdom it shall be performed.'

פֶּרֶק ו

1 בַּלַּיְלָה הַהוּא נָדְדָה שְׁנַת הַמֶּלֶךְ וַיֹּאמֶר לְהָבִיא אֶת־סֵפֶר הַזִּכְרֹנוֹת דִּבְרֵי הַיָּמִים וַיִּהְיוּ נִקְרָאִים לִפְנֵי הַמֶּלֶךְ. **2** וַיִּמָּצֵא כָתוּב אֲשֶׁר הִגִּיד מָרְדֳּכַי עַל־בִּגְתָנָא וָתֶרֶשׁ שְׁנֵי סָרִיסֵי הַמֶּלֶךְ מִשֹּׁמְרֵי הַסַּף אֲשֶׁר בִּקְשׁוּ לִשְׁלֹחַ יָד בַּמֶּלֶךְ אֲחַשְׁוֵרוֹשׁ. **3** וַיֹּאמֶר הַמֶּלֶךְ מַה־נַּעֲשָׂה יְקָר וּגְדוּלָּה לְמָרְדֳּכַי עַל־זֶה וַיֹּאמְרוּ נַעֲרֵי הַמֶּלֶךְ מְשָׁרְתָיו לֹא־נַעֲשָׂה עִמּוֹ דָּבָר. **4** וַיֹּאמֶר הַמֶּלֶךְ מִי בֶחָצֵר

וְהָמָן בָּא לַחֲצַר בֵּית־הַמֶּלֶךְ הַחִיצוֹנָה לֵאמֹר
לַמֶּלֶךְ לִתְלוֹת אֶת־מָרְדֳּכַי עַל־הָעֵץ אֲשֶׁר־הֵכִין לוֹ.

5 וַיֹּאמְרוּ נַעֲרֵי הַמֶּלֶךְ אֵלָיו הִנֵּה הָמָן עֹמֵד בֶּחָצֵר וַיֹּאמֶר הַמֶּלֶךְ יָבוֹא. **6** וַיָּבוֹא הָמָן וַיֹּאמֶר לוֹ הַמֶּלֶךְ מַה־לַּעֲשׂוֹת בָּאִישׁ אֲשֶׁר הַמֶּלֶךְ חָפֵץ בִּיקָרוֹ

וַיֹּאמֶר הָמָן בְּלִבּוֹ לְמִי יַחְפֹּץ הַמֶּלֶךְ לַעֲשׂוֹת
יְקָר יוֹתֵר מִמֶּנִּי.

7 וַיֹּאמֶר הָמָן אֶל־הַמֶּלֶךְ אִישׁ אֲשֶׁר הַמֶּלֶךְ חָפֵץ בִּיקָרוֹ. **8** יָבִיאוּ לְבוּשׁ מַלְכוּת אֲשֶׁר לָבַשׁ־בּוֹ הַמֶּלֶךְ וְסוּס אֲשֶׁר רָכַב עָלָיו הַמֶּלֶךְ וַאֲשֶׁר נִתַּן כֶּתֶר מַלְכוּת בְּרֹאשׁוֹ. **9** וְנָתוֹן הַלְּבוּשׁ וְהַסּוּס עַל־יַד־אִישׁ מִשָּׂרֵי הַמֶּלֶךְ הַפַּרְתְּמִים וְהִלְבִּישׁוּ אֶת־הָאִישׁ אֲשֶׁר הַמֶּלֶךְ חָפֵץ בִּיקָרוֹ וְהִרְכִּיבֻהוּ עַל־הַסּוּס בִּרְחוֹב הָעִיר וְקָרְאוּ לְפָנָיו כָּכָה יֵעָשֶׂה לָאִישׁ אֲשֶׁר הַמֶּלֶךְ חָפֵץ בִּיקָרוֹ. **10** וַיֹּאמֶר הַמֶּלֶךְ לְהָמָן מַהֵר קַח אֶת־הַלְּבוּשׁ וְאֶת־הַסּוּס כַּאֲשֶׁר דִּבַּרְתָּ וַעֲשֵׂה־כֵן לְמָרְדֳּכַי הַיְּהוּדִי הַיּוֹשֵׁב בְּשַׁעַר הַמֶּלֶךְ אַל־תַּפֵּל דָּבָר מִכֹּל אֲשֶׁר דִּבַּרְתָּ. **11** וַיִּקַּח הָמָן אֶת־הַלְּבוּשׁ וְאֶת־הַסּוּס וַיַּלְבֵּשׁ אֶת־מָרְדֳּכַי וַיַּרְכִּיבֵהוּ בִּרְחוֹב הָעִיר וַיִּקְרָא לְפָנָיו כָּכָה יֵעָשֶׂה לָאִישׁ אֲשֶׁר הַמֶּלֶךְ חָפֵץ בִּיקָרוֹ. **12** וַיָּשָׁב מָרְדֳּכַי אֶל־שַׁעַר הַמֶּלֶךְ; וְהָמָן נִדְחַף אֶל־בֵּיתוֹ אָבֵל וַחֲפוּי רֹאשׁ. **13** וַיְסַפֵּר הָמָן לְזֶרֶשׁ אִשְׁתּוֹ וּלְכָל־אֹהֲבָיו אֵת כָּל־אֲשֶׁר קָרָהוּ וַיֹּאמְרוּ לוֹ חֲכָמָיו וְזֶרֶשׁ אִשְׁתּוֹ אִם מִזֶּרַע הַיְּהוּדִים מָרְדֳּכַי אֲשֶׁר הַחִלּוֹתָ לִנְפֹּל לְפָנָיו לֹא־תוּכַל לוֹ כִּי־נָפוֹל תִּפּוֹל לְפָנָיו. **14** עוֹדָם מְדַבְּרִים עִמּוֹ וְסָרִיסֵי הַמֶּלֶךְ הִגִּיעוּ וַיַּבְהִלוּ לְהָבִיא אֶת־הָמָן אֶל־הַמִּשְׁתֶּה אֲשֶׁר־עָשְׂתָה אֶסְתֵּר.

פֶּרֶק ז

1 וַיָּבֹא הַמֶּלֶךְ וְהָמָן לִשְׁתּוֹת עִם־אֶסְתֵּר הַמַּלְכָּה. **2** וַיֹּאמֶר הַמֶּלֶךְ לְאֶסְתֵּר גַּם בַּיּוֹם הַשֵּׁנִי בְּמִשְׁתֵּה הַיַּיִן מַה־שְּׁאֵלָתֵךְ אֶסְתֵּר הַמַּלְכָּה וְתִנָּתֵן לָךְ וּמַה־בַּקָּשָׁתֵךְ עַד־חֲצִי הַמַּלְכוּת וְתֵעָשׂ.

3 Then Queen Esther answered and said: 'If I have found favour in thy sight O king and if it please the king, let my life be given me at my petition, and my people at my request; **4** for we are sold, I and my people, to be destroyed, to be slain and to perish. If we were only to be sold for bondmen and bondwomen, I would have held my peace for the adversary is not worth distressing the king for.' [S]

5 Then spoke King Ahasuerus and said unto Esther the queen: 'Who is he and where is he that durst presume in his heart to do so?' **6** And Esther said: 'An adversary and an enemy: even this wicked **Haman**.' Then **Haman** was terrified before the king and the queen. **7** And the king arose in his wrath from the feast of wine and went into the palace garden but **Haman** remained to beg Esther the queen for his life, for he saw that there was evil determined against him by the king. **8** Then the king returned from the palace garden to the place of the party of wine and **Haman** was fallen on the couch on which Esther was. Then said the king: 'Will he even assault the queen before me in the house?' As the word went out of the king's mouth they covered **Haman**'s face. **9** Then said Harvonah, one of the chamberlains that were before the king: 'See also the gallows fifty cubits high that **Haman** made for Mordecai who spoke good for the king standeth in the house of **Haman**.' And the king said: 'Hang him thereon.' **10** So they hanged **Haman** on the gallows that he had prepared for Mordecai. Then was the king's wrath assuaged. [S]

Chapter 8

1 On that day did King Ahasuerus give to Esther the Queen the house of **Haman**, the enemy of the Jews. And Mordecai did attend the king, for Esther had explained what he was unto her. **2** And the king took off his ring which he had taken from **Haman** and gave it unto Mordecai.

And Esther set Mordecai over the house of **Haman**. [S]

3 And Esther spoke yet again before the king and fell down at his feet and besought him with tears to put away the mischief of **Haman** the Agagite and his plan that he had devised against the Jews.

4 Then the king held out to Esther the golden sceptre, so Esther arose and stood before the king. **5** And she said: 'If

it please the king and if I have found favour in his sight, and	the thing seem right before the king and I be pleasing in his eyes

be it written to reverse the documents devised by **Haman** the son of Hammedatha the Agagite that he wrote to destroy the Jews in all the king's provinces

6 for how can I endure to see the evil that shall come unto my people?'	or how can I endure to see the destruction of my kindred?' [S]

7 Then King Ahasuerus said unto Queen Esther and to Mordecai the Jew: 'Behold I have given Esther the house of **Haman** and they have hanged him on the gallows because he laid his hand upon the Jews. **8** Write ye also concerning the Jews as it pleaseth you in the king's name and seal it with the king's ring for no man may reverse the writing which is written in the king's name and sealed with the king's ring.' **9** Then were the king's scribes called at that time in the third month which is the month of Sivan on the twenty-third day thereof and it was written according to all that Mordecai commanded

3 וַתַּעַן אֶסְתֵּר הַמַּלְכָּה וַתֹּאמַר אִם־מָצָאתִי חֵן בְּעֵינֶיךָ הַמֶּלֶךְ וְאִם־עַל־הַמֶּלֶךְ טוֹב תִּנָּתֶן־לִי נַפְשִׁי בִּשְׁאֵלָתִי וְעַמִּי בְּבַקָּשָׁתִי. 4 כִּי נִמְכַּרְנוּ אֲנִי וְעַמִּי לְהַשְׁמִיד לַהֲרוֹג וּלְאַבֵּד; וְאִלּוּ לַעֲבָדִים וְלִשְׁפָחוֹת נִמְכַּרְנוּ הֶחֱרַשְׁתִּי כִּי אֵין הַצָּר שֹׁוֶה בְּנֵזֶק הַמֶּלֶךְ. [ס]

5 וַיֹּאמֶר הַמֶּלֶךְ אֲחַשְׁוֵרוֹשׁ וַיֹּאמֶר לְאֶסְתֵּר הַמַּלְכָּה מִי הוּא זֶה וְאֵי־זֶה הוּא אֲשֶׁר־מְלָאוֹ לִבּוֹ לַעֲשׂוֹת כֵּן. 6 וַתֹּאמֶר אֶסְתֵּר אִישׁ צַר וְאוֹיֵב הָמָן הָרָע הַזֶּה וְהָמָן נִבְעַת מִלִּפְנֵי הַמֶּלֶךְ וְהַמַּלְכָּה. 7 וְהַמֶּלֶךְ קָם בַּחֲמָתוֹ מִמִּשְׁתֵּה הַיַּיִן אֶל־גִּנַּת הַבִּיתָן וְהָמָן עָמַד לְבַקֵּשׁ עַל־נַפְשׁוֹ מֵאֶסְתֵּר הַמַּלְכָּה כִּי רָאָה כִּי־כָלְתָה אֵלָיו הָרָעָה מֵאֵת הַמֶּלֶךְ. 8 וְהַמֶּלֶךְ שָׁב מִגִּנַּת הַבִּיתָן אֶל־בֵּית מִשְׁתֵּה הַיַּיִן וְהָמָן נֹפֵל עַל־הַמִּטָּה אֲשֶׁר אֶסְתֵּר עָלֶיהָ וַיֹּאמֶר הַמֶּלֶךְ הֲגַם לִכְבּוֹשׁ אֶת־הַמַּלְכָּה עִמִּי בַּבָּיִת הַדָּבָר יָצָא מִפִּי הַמֶּלֶךְ וּפְנֵי הָמָן חָפוּ. 9 וַיֹּאמֶר חַרְבוֹנָה אֶחָד מִן־הַסָּרִיסִים לִפְנֵי הַמֶּלֶךְ גַּם הִנֵּה־הָעֵץ אֲשֶׁר־עָשָׂה הָמָן לְמָרְדֳּכַי אֲשֶׁר דִּבֶּר־טוֹב עַל־הַמֶּלֶךְ עֹמֵד בְּבֵית הָמָן גָּבֹהַּ חֲמִשִּׁים אַמָּה וַיֹּאמֶר הַמֶּלֶךְ תְּלֻהוּ עָלָיו. 10 וַיִּתְלוּ אֶת־הָמָן עַל־הָעֵץ אֲשֶׁר־הֵכִין לְמָרְדֳּכָי וַחֲמַת הַמֶּלֶךְ שָׁכָכָה. [ס]

פֶּרֶק ח

1 בַּיּוֹם הַהוּא נָתַן הַמֶּלֶךְ אֲחַשְׁוֵרוֹשׁ לְאֶסְתֵּר הַמַּלְכָּה אֶת־בֵּית הָמָן צֹרֵר הַיְּהוּדִיים (הַיְּהוּדִים) וּמָרְדֳּכַי בָּא לִפְנֵי הַמֶּלֶךְ כִּי־הִגִּידָה אֶסְתֵּר מַה הוּא־לָהּ. 2 וַיָּסַר הַמֶּלֶךְ אֶת־טַבַּעְתּוֹ אֲשֶׁר הֶעֱבִיר מֵהָמָן וַיִּתְּנָהּ לְמָרְדֳּכַי

וַתָּשֶׂם אֶסְתֵּר אֶת־מָרְדֳּכַי עַל־בֵּית הָמָן. [ס]

3 וַתּוֹסֶף אֶסְתֵּר וַתְּדַבֵּר לִפְנֵי הַמֶּלֶךְ וַתִּפֹּל לִפְנֵי הַמֶּלֶךְ וַתֵּבְךְּ וַתִּתְחַנֶּן־לוֹ לְהַעֲבִיר אֶת־רָעַת הָמָן הָאֲגָגִי וְאֵת מַחֲשַׁבְתּוֹ אֲשֶׁר חָשַׁב עַל־הַיְּהוּדִים. 4 וַיּוֹשֶׁט הַמֶּלֶךְ לְאֶסְתֵּר אֵת שַׁרְבִט הַזָּהָב וַתָּקָם אֶסְתֵּר וַתַּעֲמֹד לִפְנֵי הַמֶּלֶךְ. 5 וַתֹּאמֶר אִם־עַל־הַמֶּלֶךְ טוֹב וְאִם־מָצָאתִי חֵן לְפָנָיו וְ־ כָּשֵׁר הַדָּבָר לִפְנֵי הַמֶּלֶךְ וְטוֹבָה אֲנִי בְּעֵינָיו

יִכָּתֵב לְהָשִׁיב אֶת־הַסְּפָרִים מַחֲשֶׁבֶת הָמָן בֶּן־ הַמְּדָתָא הָאֲגָגִי אֲשֶׁר כָּתַב לְאַבֵּד אֶת־הַיְּהוּדִים אֲשֶׁר בְּכָל־מְדִינוֹת הַמֶּלֶךְ.

6 כִּי אֵיכָכָה אוּכַל וְרָאִיתִי בָּרָעָה אֲשֶׁר־ יִמְצָא אֶת־עַמִּי וְאֵיכָכָה אוּכַל וְרָאִיתִי בְּאָבְדַן מוֹלַדְתִּי. [ס]

7 וַיֹּאמֶר הַמֶּלֶךְ אֲחַשְׁוֵרֹשׁ לְאֶסְתֵּר הַמַּלְכָּה וּלְמָרְדֳּכַי הַיְּהוּדִי הִנֵּה בֵית־הָמָן נָתַתִּי לְאֶסְתֵּר וְאֹתוֹ תָּלוּ עַל־הָעֵץ עַל אֲשֶׁר־שָׁלַח יָדוֹ בַּיְּהוּדִיים (בַּיְּהוּדִים). 8 וְאַתֶּם כִּתְבוּ עַל־הַיְּהוּדִים כַּטּוֹב בְּעֵינֵיכֶם בְּשֵׁם הַמֶּלֶךְ וְחִתְמוּ בְּטַבַּעַת הַמֶּלֶךְ כִּי־כְתָב אֲשֶׁר־נִכְתָּב בְּשֵׁם־הַמֶּלֶךְ וְנַחְתּוֹם בְּטַבַּעַת הַמֶּלֶךְ אֵין לְהָשִׁיב. 9 וַיִּקָּרְאוּ סֹפְרֵי־הַמֶּלֶךְ בָּעֵת־הַהִיא בַּחֹדֶשׁ הַשְּׁלִישִׁי הוּא־חֹדֶשׁ סִיוָן בִּשְׁלוֹשָׁה וְעֶשְׂרִים בּוֹ וַיִּכָּתֵב כְּכָל־אֲשֶׁר־צִוָּה מָרְדֳּכַי

| to the Jews and | to the satraps and governors and princes of the provinces which are from India unto Ethiopia a hundred and twenty seven provinces, | unto every province according to the writing thereof and unto every people after their language, and | to the Jews according to their writing, and according to their language. |

10 And they wrote in the name of King Ahasuerus and sealed it with the king's ring

and sent letters by posts on horseback riding on swift steeds used in the king's service bred of the stud **11** that the king had let the Jews that were in every city gather together and stand for their life to destroy, slay and cause to perish all the forces of the people and province that would assault them, their little ones and women, and take the spoil of them for a prey **12** on one day in all the provinces of King Ahasuerus, namely on the thirteenth day of the twelfth month (which is the month Adar).

13 The copy of the writing to be given out for a decree in every province was to be published unto all the peoples and that the Jews should be ready against that day to avenge themselves on their enemies.

14 So the posts that rode upon swift steeds that were used in the king's service went out, hastened and pressed on by the king's commandment, and the decree was given out in Shushan fortress. [S]

15 And Mordecai went forth from the presence of the king in royal apparel of blue and white and with a great crown of gold and with a robe of fine linen and purple, and the city of Shushan shouted and was glad. 16 The Jews had light and gladness and joy and honour. 17 And in every province and in every city whithersoever the king's commandment and his decree came the Jews had gladness and joy, a feast and a festival. And many from among the peoples of the land became Jews

for the fear of the Jews was fallen upon them.

Chapter 9

1 Now in the twelfth month which is the month Adar on the thirteenth day of the same when the king's command and his decree drew near to be carried out

in the day that the enemies of the Jews hoped to have rule over them

whereas it was turned to the contrary that the Jews had rule over them that hated them,

2 the Jews gathered together in their cities throughout all the provinces of King Ahasuerus to lay hand on such as wanted to hurt them, and no man could withstand them

for the fear of them was fallen upon all the peoples.

3 And all the princes of the provinces and the satraps and the governors and they that did the king's business helped the Jews

for the fear of Mordecai was fallen upon them

4 For Mordecai was great in the king's house and his fame went forth throughout all the provinces.

For the man Mordecai was becoming great.

אֶל הָאֲחַשְׁדַּרְפְּנִים | מְדִינָה וּמְדִינָה | וְאֶל־הַיְּהוּדִים
וְהַפַּחוֹת וְשָׂרֵי | כִּכְתָבָהּ וְעַם וָעָם | כִּכְתָבָם וְכִלְשֹׁנָם.
הַמְּדִינוֹת אֲשֶׁר מֵהֹדּוּ | כִּלְשֹׁנוֹ |
וְעַד־כּוּשׁ שֶׁבַע וְעֶשְׂרִים | |
וּמֵאָה מְדִינָה | | אֶל־הַיְּהוּדִים וְ

10 וַיִּכְתֹּב בְּשֵׁם הַמֶּלֶךְ אֲחַשְׁוֵרֹשׁ וַיַּחְתֹּם בְּטַבַּעַת הַמֶּלֶךְ

וַיִּשְׁלַח סְפָרִים בְּיַד הָרָצִים בַּסּוּסִים רֹכְבֵי
הָרֶכֶשׁ הָאֲחַשְׁתְּרָנִים בְּנֵי הָרַמָּכִים. 11 אֲשֶׁר נָתַן
הַמֶּלֶךְ לַיְּהוּדִים אֲשֶׁר בְּכָל־עִיר־וָעִיר לְהִקָּהֵל
וְלַעֲמֹד עַל־נַפְשָׁם לְהַשְׁמִיד וְלַהֲרֹג וּלְאַבֵּד אֶת־
כָּל־חֵיל עַם וּמְדִינָה הַצָּרִים אֹתָם טַף וְנָשִׁים
וּשְׁלָלָם לָבוֹז. 12 בְּיוֹם אֶחָד בְּכָל־מְדִינוֹת הַמֶּלֶךְ
אֲחַשְׁוֵרוֹשׁ בִּשְׁלוֹשָׁה עָשָׂר לְחֹדֶשׁ שְׁנֵים־עָשָׂר
הוּא־חֹדֶשׁ אֲדָר.

13 פַּתְשֶׁגֶן הַכְּתָב
לְהִנָּתֵן דָּת בְּכָל־
מְדִינָה וּמְדִינָה גָּלוּי
לְכָל־הָעַמִּים וְלִהְיוֹת
הַיְּהוּדִיים (הַיְּהוּדִים)
עֲתוּדִים (עֲתִידִים)
לַיּוֹם הַזֶּה לְהִנָּקֵם
מֵאֹיְבֵיהֶם.

14 הָרָצִים רֹכְבֵי
הָרֶכֶשׁ הָאֲחַשְׁתְּרָנִים
יָצְאוּ מְבֹהָלִים
וּדְחוּפִים בִּדְבַר הַמֶּלֶךְ
וְהַדָּת נִתְּנָה בְּשׁוּשַׁן
הַבִּירָה. [ס]

15 וּמָרְדֳּכַי יָצָא מִלִּפְנֵי הַמֶּלֶךְ בִּלְבוּשׁ מַלְכוּת תְּכֵלֶת וָחוּר וַעֲטֶרֶת זָהָב גְּדוֹלָה וְתַכְרִיךְ בּוּץ
וְאַרְגָּמָן וְהָעִיר שׁוּשָׁן צָהֲלָה וְשָׂמֵחָה. 16 לַיְּהוּדִים הָיְתָה אוֹרָה וְשִׂמְחָה וְשָׂשֹׂן וִיקָר.
17 וּבְכָל־מְדִינָה וּמְדִינָה וּבְכָל־עִיר וָעִיר מְקוֹם אֲשֶׁר דְּבַר־הַמֶּלֶךְ וְדָתוֹ מַגִּיעַ שִׂמְחָה וְשָׂשׂוֹן
לַיְּהוּדִים מִשְׁתֶּה וְיוֹם טוֹב וְרַבִּים מֵעַמֵּי הָאָרֶץ מִתְיַהֲדִים

כִּי־נָפַל פַּחַד־הַיְּהוּדִים עֲלֵיהֶם.

פֶּרֶק ט

1 וּבִשְׁנֵים עָשָׂר חֹדֶשׁ הוּא־חֹדֶשׁ אֲדָר בִּשְׁלוֹשָׁה עָשָׂר יוֹם בּוֹ אֲשֶׁר
הִגִּיעַ דְּבַר־הַמֶּלֶךְ וְדָתוֹ לְהֵעָשׂוֹת

בַּיּוֹם אֲשֶׁר שִׂבְּרוּ אֹיְבֵי הַיְּהוּדִים לִשְׁלוֹט | וְנַהֲפוֹךְ הוּא אֲשֶׁר יִשְׁלְטוּ הַיְּהוּדִים הֵמָּה
בָּהֶם | בְּשֹׂנְאֵיהֶם.

2 נִקְהֲלוּ הַיְּהוּדִים בְּעָרֵיהֶם בְּכָל־מְדִינוֹת הַמֶּלֶךְ אֲחַשְׁוֵרוֹשׁ לִשְׁלֹחַ יָד בִּמְבַקְשֵׁי רָעָתָם
וְאִישׁ לֹא־עָמַד לִפְנֵיהֶם

כִּי־נָפַל פַּחְדָּם עַל־כָּל־הָעַמִּים.

3 וְכָל־שָׂרֵי הַמְּדִינוֹת וְהָאֲחַשְׁדַּרְפְּנִים וְהַפַּחוֹת וְעֹשֵׂי הַמְּלָאכָה אֲשֶׁר לַמֶּלֶךְ מְנַשְּׂאִים אֶת־הַיְּהוּדִים

כִּי־נָפַל פַּחַד־מָרְדֳּכַי עֲלֵיהֶם.

4 כִּי־גָדוֹל מָרְדֳּכַי בְּבֵית הַמֶּלֶךְ וְשָׁמְעוֹ הוֹלֵךְ | כִּי־הָאִישׁ מָרְדֳּכַי הוֹלֵךְ וְגָדוֹל.
בְּכָל־הַמְּדִינוֹת:

5 And the Jews smote all their enemies with the stroke of the sword and with slaughter and destruction and did what they would unto them that hated them. **6** And in Shushan fortress the Jews slew and destroyed five hundred men. [S]

7 And slew Parshandatha [S] and Dalphon [S] and Aspatha [S] **8** and Poratha [S] and Adalia [S] and Aridatha [S] **9** and Parmashta [S] and Arisai [S] and Aridai [S] and Vaizatha, [S] **10** the ten sons of **Haman** the son of Hammedatha, the Jews' enemy.

11 On that day the number of those slain in Shushan fortress was brought before the king. **12** And the king said unto Queen Esther: 'In Shushan fortress the Jews have slain and destroyed five hundred men:

plus the ten sons of **Haman**;	what then have they done in the rest of the king's provinces!'

now whatever thy plea it shall be granted thee and whatever thy request further it shall be done.' **13** Then said Esther: 'If the king wilt,

'let the Jews in Shushan do tomorrow also as today's decree'	'also let **Haman**'s ten sons be hanged upon the gallows'
14 and the king ordered it so to be done.	And a decree was given out in Shushan and they hanged **Haman**'s ten sons.
15 And the Jews that were in Shushan gathered also on the fourteenth day of the month of Adar and slew three hundred men in Shushan	**16** And the other Jews that were in the king's provinces gathered on the thirteenth day of the month of Adar and stood for their lives and relieved themselves of their enemies and slew of them that hated them seventy-five thousand
but on the spoil they laid not their hand.	*but on the spoil they laid not their hand.*
	17 This was on the thirteenth day of the month Adar, and *they rested on the fourteenth day of the same and made it a day of feasting and joy.*
18 [In summary,] the Jews that were in Shushan gathered on the thirteenth day thereof and on the fourteenth thereof, and *they rested on the fifteenth day of the same and made it a day of feasting and joy.*	**19** That is why the Jews of the villages that dwell in the unwalled towns *make the fourteenth day of the month Adar a day of joy and feasting* and a festival and of sending portions one to another.

20 And Mordecai wrote these things and sent letters unto all the Jews in all the provinces of King Ahasuerus both nigh and far **21** to enjoin them to keep the fourteenth day of the month of Adar and the fifteenth day of the same every

5 וַיַּכּוּ הַיְּהוּדִים בְּכָל־אֹיְבֵיהֶם מַכַּת־חֶרֶב וְהֶרֶג וְאַבְדָן וַיַּעֲשׂוּ בְשֹׂנְאֵיהֶם
כִּרְצוֹנָם. **6** וּבְשׁוּשַׁן הַבִּירָה הָרְגוּ הַיְּהוּדִים וְאַבֵּד חֲמֵשׁ מֵאוֹת אִישׁ. [ס]

7 וְאֵת [ר] פַּרְשַׁנְדָּתָא [ס] וְאֵת [ר] דַּלְפוֹן [ס] וְאֵת [ר] אַסְפָּתָא. [ס]

8 וְאֵת [ר] פּוֹרָתָא [ס] וְאֵת [ר] אֲדַלְיָא [ס] וְאֵת [ר] אֲרִידָתָא. [ס]

9 וְאֵת [ר] פַּרְמַשְׁתָּא [ס] וְאֵת [ר] אֲרִיסַי [ס] וְאֵת [ר] אֲרִדַי [ס] וְאֵת

[ר] וַיְזָתָא. [ס] **10** עֲשֶׂרֶת בְּנֵי הָמָן בֶּן־הַמְּדָתָא צֹרֵר הַיְּהוּדִים הָרָגוּ.

11 בַּיּוֹם הַהוּא בָּא מִסְפַּר הַהֲרוּגִים בְּשׁוּשַׁן הַבִּירָה לִפְנֵי הַמֶּלֶךְ. **12** וַיֹּאמֶר הַמֶּלֶךְ לְאֶסְתֵּר
הַמַּלְכָּה בְּשׁוּשַׁן הַבִּירָה הָרְגוּ הַיְּהוּדִים וְאַבֵּד חֲמֵשׁ מֵאוֹת אִישׁ

| בִּשְׁאָר מְדִינוֹת הַמֶּלֶךְ | וְאֵת עֲשֶׂרֶת בְּנֵי־הָמָן |
| מֶה עָשׂוּ | |

וּמַה־שְּׁאֵלָתֵךְ וְיִנָּתֵן לָךְ וּמַה־בַּקָּשָׁתֵךְ עוֹד וְתֵעָשׂ. **13** וַתֹּאמֶר אֶסְתֵּר אִם־עַל־הַמֶּלֶךְ טוֹב

| וְאֵת עֲשֶׂרֶת בְּנֵי־הָמָן יִתְלוּ עַל־הָעֵץ. | יִנָּתֵן גַּם־מָחָר לַיְּהוּדִים אֲשֶׁר בְּשׁוּשָׁן לַעֲשׂוֹת |
| | כְּדָת הַיּוֹם |

| וַתִּנָּתֵן דָּת בְּשׁוּשָׁן וְאֵת עֲשֶׂרֶת | **14** וַיֹּאמֶר הַמֶּלֶךְ לְהֵעָשׂוֹת כֵּן |
| בְּנֵי־הָמָן תָּלוּ. | |

16 וּשְׁאָר הַיְּהוּדִים אֲשֶׁר בִּמְדִינוֹת	**15** וַיִּקָּהֲלוּ הַיְּהוּדִיים (הַיְּהוּדִים)
הַמֶּלֶךְ נִקְהֲלוּ וְעָמֹד עַל־נַפְשָׁם וְנוֹחַ	אֲשֶׁר־בְּשׁוּשָׁן גַּם בְּיוֹם אַרְבָּעָה עָשָׂר
מֵאֹיְבֵיהֶם וְהָרוֹג בְּשֹׂנְאֵיהֶם חֲמִשָּׁה	לְחֹדֶשׁ אֲדָר וַיַּהַרְגוּ בְשׁוּשָׁן שְׁלֹשׁ
וְשִׁבְעִים אָלֶף	מֵאוֹת אִישׁ

| וּבַבִּזָּה לֹא שָׁלְחוּ אֶת־יָדָם. | וּבַבִּזָּה לֹא שָׁלְחוּ אֶת־יָדָם. |

17 בְּיוֹם־שְׁלוֹשָׁה עָשָׂר לְחֹדֶשׁ אֲדָר וְנוֹחַ בְּאַרְבָּעָה
עָשָׂר בּוֹ וְעָשֹׂה אֹתוֹ יוֹם מִשְׁתֶּה וְשִׂמְחָה.

19 עַל־כֵּן הַיְּהוּדִים הַפְּרוֹזִים (הַפְּרָזִים) הַיֹּשְׁבִים	**18** וְהַיְּהוּדִיים (וְהַיְּהוּדִים) אֲשֶׁר־בְּשׁוּשָׁן
בְּעָרֵי הַפְּרָזוֹת עֹשִׂים אֵת יוֹם אַרְבָּעָה עָשָׂר	נִקְהֲלוּ בִּשְׁלוֹשָׁה עָשָׂר בּוֹ וּבְאַרְבָּעָה עָשָׂר
לְחֹדֶשׁ אֲדָר שִׂמְחָה וּמִשְׁתֶּה וְיוֹם טוֹב וּמִשְׁלֹחַ	בּוֹ וְנוֹחַ בַּחֲמִשָּׁה עָשָׂר בּוֹ וְעָשֹׂה אֹתוֹ יוֹם
מָנוֹת אִישׁ לְרֵעֵהוּ.	מִשְׁתֶּה וְשִׂמְחָה.

20 וַיִּכְתֹּב מָרְדֳּכַי אֶת־הַדְּבָרִים הָאֵלֶּה וַיִּשְׁלַח
סְפָרִים אֶל־כָּל־הַיְּהוּדִים אֲשֶׁר בְּכָל־מְדִינוֹת
הַמֶּלֶךְ אֲחַשְׁוֵרוֹשׁ הַקְּרוֹבִים וְהָרְחוֹקִים. **21** לְקַיֵּם
עֲלֵיהֶם לִהְיוֹת עֹשִׂים אֵת יוֹם אַרְבָּעָה עָשָׂר

year, **22** the days wherein the Jews had rest from their enemies and the month which was turned unto them from sorrow to joy and from mourning into a festival, that they should make them days of feasting and joy and of sending portions one to another and gifts to the poor. **23** And the Jews took upon them to do as they had begun and as Mordecai had written unto them **24** since **Haman** the son of Hammedatha the Agagite, the enemy of all the Jews, had plotted against the Jews to destroy them and had cast *pur*

—i.e, the *lot*—

to discomfit them and to destroy them.

25 [In summary,] when *she* [i.e. Esther] came before the king he commanded by letters that his [i.e. Haman's] wicked plan which he had devised against the Jews should return upon his own head and that he and his sons should be hanged on the gallows.

26 Therefore they called these days Purim after the name of the *pur.*

And so because of all the words of this letter and of what they had seen concerning this matter and what had come unto them **27** the Jews ordained and took upon them and upon their seed and upon all who joined themselves unto them so that it should not fail that they would keep these two days according to the writing thereof and according to the appointed time thereof each year **28** and that these days should be remembered and kept throughout every generation, every family, every province and every city and that these days of Purim should not fail from among the Jews nor the memorial of them perish from their seed. [S]

29 Then wrote Queen Esther, daughter of Abihail,

(and of Mordecai the Jew)

by all her authority

(to confirm this second letter of Purim)

לְחֹדֶשׁ אֲדָר וְאֵת יוֹם־חֲמִשָּׁה עָשָׂר בּוֹ בְּכָל־
שָׁנָה וְשָׁנָה. **22** כַּיָּמִים אֲשֶׁר־נָחוּ בָהֶם הַיְּהוּדִים
מֵאֹיְבֵיהֶם וְהַחֹדֶשׁ אֲשֶׁר נֶהְפַּךְ לָהֶם מִיָּגוֹן
לְשִׂמְחָה וּמֵאֵבֶל לְיוֹם טוֹב לַעֲשׂוֹת אוֹתָם יְמֵי
מִשְׁתֶּה וְשִׂמְחָה וּמִשְׁלֹחַ מָנוֹת אִישׁ לְרֵעֵהוּ
וּמַתָּנוֹת לָאֶבְיֹנִים. **23** וְקִבֵּל הַיְּהוּדִים אֵת
אֲשֶׁר־הֵחֵלּוּ לַעֲשׂוֹת וְאֵת אֲשֶׁר־כָּתַב מָרְדֳּכַי
אֲלֵיהֶם. **24** כִּי הָמָן בֶּן־הַמְּדָתָא הָאֲגָגִי צֹרֵר כָּל־
הַיְּהוּדִים חָשַׁב עַל־הַיְּהוּדִים לְאַבְּדָם וְהִפִּל פּוּר

הוּא הַגּוֹרָל |

לְהֻמָּם וּלְאַבְּדָם.

25 וּבְבֹאָהּ לִפְנֵי הַמֶּלֶךְ אָמַר עִם־
הַסֵּפֶר יָשׁוּב מַחֲשַׁבְתּוֹ הָרָעָה אֲשֶׁר־
חָשַׁב עַל־הַיְּהוּדִים עַל־רֹאשׁוֹ וְתָלוּ
אֹתוֹ וְאֶת־בָּנָיו עַל־הָעֵץ.

26 עַל־כֵּן קָרְאוּ
לַיָּמִים הָאֵלֶּה פוּרִים
עַל־שֵׁם הַפּוּר

עַל־כֵּן עַל־כָּל־דִּבְרֵי הָאִגֶּרֶת הַזֹּאת וּמָה־רָאוּ
עַל־כָּכָה וּמָה הִגִּיעַ אֲלֵיהֶם. **27** קִיְּמוּ וְקִבֵּל
(וְקִבְּלוּ) הַיְּהוּדִים עֲלֵיהֶם וְעַל־זַרְעָם וְעַל
כָּל־הַנִּלְוִים עֲלֵיהֶם וְלֹא יַעֲבוֹר לִהְיוֹת עֹשִׂים
אֵת שְׁנֵי הַיָּמִים הָאֵלֶּה כִּכְתָבָם וְכִזְמַנָּם
בְּכָל־שָׁנָה וְשָׁנָה. **28** וְהַיָּמִים הָאֵלֶּה נִזְכָּרִים
וְנַעֲשִׂים בְּכָל־דּוֹר וָדוֹר מִשְׁפָּחָה וּמִשְׁפָּחָה
מְדִינָה וּמְדִינָה וְעִיר וָעִיר וִימֵי הַפּוּרִים
הָאֵלֶּה לֹא יַעַבְרוּ מִתּוֹךְ הַיְּהוּדִים וְזִכְרָם לֹא־
יָסוּף מִזַּרְעָם. [ס]

29 וַתִּכְתֹּב אֶסְתֵּר הַמַּלְכָּה בַת־אֲבִיחַיִל

וּמָרְדֳּכַי הַיְּהוּדִי

אֶת־כָּל־תֹּקֶף

לְקַיֵּם אֵת אִגֶּרֶת הַפֻּרִים הַזֹּאת הַשֵּׁנִית

30 And *he sent* letters

unto all the Jews

to the hundred and twenty-seven provinces of the kingdom of Ahasuerus

with words of peace and truth

31 to confirm these days of Purim in their appointed times according as Mordecai the Jew and Queen Esther had enjoined them

as they had ordained for themselves and for their seed the matters of the fastings and their cry **32** and the commandment of Esther confirmed these matters of Purim

and it was written in the book. [S]

Chapter 10

1 And King Ahasuerus laid a tribute upon the land and upon the isles of the sea. **2** And all the acts of his power and his might and the account of the greatness of Mordecai, whom the king promoted, are they not written in the *Book of Chronicles of the kings of Media and Persia*?
3 **For Mordecai the Jew was second unto King Ahasuerus and great to the Jews and accepted by the multitude of his brethren, seeking the good of his people and speaking peace to all his seed.**

30 וַיִּשְׁלַח סְפָרִים

אֶל־כָּל־הַיְּהוּדִים אֶל־ שֶׁבַע וְעֶשְׂרִים וּמֵאָה מְדִינָה מַלְכוּת אֲחַשְׁוֵרוֹשׁ:

דִּבְרֵי שָׁלוֹם וֶאֱמֶת.

31 לְקַיֵּם אֶת־יְמֵי הַפֻּרִים הָאֵלֶּה בִּזְמַנֵּיהֶם כַּאֲשֶׁר קִיַּם עֲלֵיהֶם מָרְדֳּכַי הַיְּהוּדִי וְאֶסְתֵּר הַמַּלְכָּה דִּבְרֵי הַצּוֹמוֹת וְזַעֲקָתָם.

וְכַאֲשֶׁר קִיְּמוּ עַל־נַפְשָׁם וְעַל־זַרְעָם **32** וּמַאֲמַר אֶסְתֵּר קִיַּם דִּבְרֵי הַפֻּרִים הָאֵלֶּה

וְנִכְתָּב בַּסֵּפֶר. ‏[ס]

פֶּרֶק י

1 וַיָּשֶׂם הַמֶּלֶךְ אחשרש (אֲחַשְׁוֵרוֹשׁ) מַס עַל־הָאָרֶץ וְאִיֵּי הַיָּם. **2** וְכָל־מַעֲשֵׂה תָקְפּוֹ וּגְבוּרָתוֹ וּפָרָשַׁת גְּדֻלַּת מָרְדֳּכַי אֲשֶׁר גִּדְּלוֹ הַמֶּלֶךְ הֲלוֹא־הֵם כְּתוּבִים עַל־סֵפֶר דִּבְרֵי הַיָּמִים לְמַלְכֵי מָדַי וּפָרָס. **3** כִּי מָרְדֳּכַי הַיְּהוּדִי מִשְׁנֶה לַמֶּלֶךְ אֲחַשְׁוֵרוֹשׁ וְגָדוֹל לַיְּהוּדִים וְרָצוּי לְרֹב אֶחָיו דֹּרֵשׁ טוֹב לְעַמּוֹ וְדֹבֵר שָׁלוֹם לְכָל־זַרְעוֹ.

Endnotes

Chapter One

1:1–2 Textual problems begin at the very start of the Book of Esther. As a single linear narrative, the text offers a clumsy opening that ascribes to Ahasuerus various random attributes. It is more compelling to see the introduction as a compound of two separate and individually more elegant introductions. The first identifies Ahasuerus as an imperial ruler in command of 127 provinces; the second locates him as a local ruler (*melech*/king) based in Shushan. English translations commonly add a bridging word—'that'—to link these two descriptions but there is no such link in the Hebrew. The difference between line 1 and line 2 alerts us at once to two different textual approaches, the associations of which will reverberate throughout the story.

1:2 *Shushan habirah* does not mean Shushan palace but the fortress or fortified district of Shushan. The Hebrew word *birah*, from the Akkadian *birtu*, means fortress and, now, by extension, fortified city or just city.

1:3–8 The legend of Esther may be reality or myth or a mixture of the two. In either case, there is no narrative need to recall two parties—one lasting 180 days, the other lasting seven—because only one party triggered the crucial event that follows: the refusal of Vashti to appear when called on by the king. In the standard linar text, Vashti's refusal follows the seven-day party, making the 180-day party a narrative redundancy, and that is unsatisfactory for the reader. A preferable reading is that we have been given two conflicting accounts, as if one followed the other, even though each originally stood on its own—a conventional way of handling alternative accounts that cannot otherwise be resolved.

1:3–8 There is a difference in authorial tone in the descriptions of the two parties. The first, ascribed here to M, is formal and reflects the king's power but lacks detail. The second, ascribed here to E, is specifically a description of the magnificence of the event. This is a retro-projection of the tone of later M and E texts; at the start of the story, neither Mordecai nor Esther had a presence at court and what is reported must come from other sources or be the product of literary invention. (On the issue of alternative attributions, see the Introduction.) As for the identification of the party in M, there appear to be three different possibilities: reading this passage as a linear text therefore makes no sense.

1:9 Like the duplicate references to Ahasuerus's parties, the reference to Vashti's own party is extraneous and dramatically unnecessary. In the standard text it follows line 8 (E text) but may make more sense following 'And when these days were fulfilled' at the start of the M text in line 5, as here.

1:10 'When the heart of the king … '. Except for the first words 'In the seventh day', this is the first example in the text of a consensual verse, i.e. a verse with no obvious M or E affiliations.

1:10 The chamberlain Harvona appears again in 7:9 but with the Hebrew spelling of his name ending with a *hay* instead of an *aleph* as here (transliterated Harvonah). In both cases, the first letter of the name is in fact an aspirate—*chet*, not *hay*—and should be spelled Charvona(h).

1:11 The usual linear reading of this verse hides a narrative divergence. Ahasuerus's order that Vashti appear at his party has two purposes: (a) to show her wearing the royal crown, and (b) to show off her beauty. These purposes are unconnected and the two phrases have therefore been separated.

1:13–14 The king's question to the wise men who knew astrology (lit. 'the times') is followed by two unusual parentheses. These have here been separated according to their apparent E and M characteristics.

1:20 Contemporary commentators who see the *Megillah* as a myth may also regard it as a feminist text. In support of this view is the obviously fantastic idea, contained in this line, that women can be ordered (by men) to honour their husbands. Lines 1:17–18 are likewise treated as indicative of male insecurity and the wish to maintain their unequal prerogative of power. The historic absence of such commentary suggests however that the notion of line 1:20 being satiric is modern; on the other hand, we have too little historic commentary from women to establish this (not that feminist commentary necessarily emanates from women).

1:22 The phrases 'into all the king's provinces' and 'into every province' are duplicates. Attributing the first to M and the second to E (as here) is based solely on an underlying editorial assumption that where there is a choice and no other evidence, the original editors automatically put M before E.

Chapter Two

2:3 Duplication of identities plagues the Book of Esther. Here, Hegai is identified as 'the king's chamberlain, keeper of the women' (*s'riys hamelech, shomeir hanoshim*), and again in 2:15 as 'the king's chamberlain, keeper of the women' (but with a hyphen/*maqaf* connecting *s'riys-hamelech*) and simply as 'keeper of the women'

in 2:8. See also n.2:8, below. Note also that the Hebrew word for chamberlain—*s'riys*—also means eunuch, as does its Persian equivalent, and many ancient langages conflate the two meanings of eunuch and vizier or senior dignitary. Highly-placed eunuchs were also often of foreign birth or extraction, hence Mordecai's eligibility for this position at the end of the story.

2:5 This line is said out loud by everyone when the *Megillah* is read at Purim, and not just by the reader, and therefore appears here in bold. See also 8:16–17 and 10:3.

2:5–6 For uncertainties about who was carried away from Jerusalem, see the Introduction.

2:7 The identification of Esther is beset by textual difficulties. The first of these is the unexplained discrepancy in the name. Here, the first name (Hadassah, Hebrew for 'myrtle' and by extension 'compassion') has been attributed to M on the basis only that it might contain more of a memory of Jewish ancestry. Jewish Bible scholars also like to link 'Esther' etymologically to the Hebrew *l'hustir* (to hide, conceal, mask). The name can however also be regard as a derivative of Ishtar, the Babylonian goddess of love, sex, fertility and war, and has been attributed here to E only because Esther might have been considered, or might have considered herself to be, a neo-Babylonian queen. Of the four statements that follow, the third—referring to Esther's beauty—ought to have nothing to do with Mordecai's adoption of her, unless it contains a veiled suggestion that Mordecai was influenced by her physical attraction and that his behaviour was therefore not exclusively virtuous. Otherwise, this statement ought to follow on from the remarks on Esther's origins rather than interrupting them. As for those other remarks, the first explains Mordecai's relationship to Esther (they were first cousins but he was older) and the fourth is essentially a duplication of the second. Here, the phrase 'for she had neither father nor mother' has been given as an E text because it suggests less self-knowledge whereas 'when her father and mother were dead' suggests slightly more precision and therefore qualifies as an M text. (But see 2:15.)

2:8 Locations within the Book of Esther are hard to pinpoint. The text identifies (a) Shushan, which may mean the province or the city, (b) *ha'ir Shushan*, the city of Shushan (8:15), (c) *Shushan habirah*, the fortress or stronghold or castle or fortified district of Shushan (1:2 et seq. but see also n.1:2, above), (d) *beit hanashiym*, the house of women (see 2:3) or harem, (e) *beit hamelech*, the king's house (see 2:8), (f) *biytan hamelech*, the king's palace or residence or quarters (see 1:5), (g) *ginat habiytan*, the garden of the palace (7:7 and 7:8), and *sha'ar hamelech*, the king's gate (2:21). From this it would appear that although the king has absolute rule over the fortified part of Shushan, he has his own private quarters within it, and when concubines are delivered to him, they are chaperoned by the royal chamberlain Hegai who controls the women's house inside the fortress.

2:8–16 The standard linear text is problematic because it suggests that when the other candidates for Vashti's former position were rounded up and housed in the fortress of Shushan, Esther alone was immediately taken to the king's house. This is not possible if, as the text goes on to say, (a) Esther was put into the custody of Hegai who gave her pride of place in the house of women, and (b) Mordecai walked daily to the house of women to check up on her, and (c) she, like the other candidates, spent twelve months preparing for her first encounter with the king. The only obvious solution is to treat the information about her being sent to the king as a characteristically abbreviated M text and everything that follows as a characteristically more detailed and more accurate E text, based on information that Esther (or an Esther) would have known better than Mordecai (or a Mordecai). Separating the text after 'Esther was taken' (*vatilokach Esther*) also solves the problem of the otherwise redundant duplication of 'to the custody of Hegai', as well as resolving the question of who is meant by 'the maiden pleased him' (*hatitav hana'arah v'einav*). As an M text, the him is Ahasuerus; as an E text it is Hegai.

2:10 That Esther did not reveal her origins is also stated at 2:20. There, however, it is accompanied by the comment that she was as obedient to Mordecai when under Hegai's charge as she had been when she was a child. Although this boast could equally be attributed to Mordecai or Esther (see Introduction), it has been given here to M.

2:11 The observation about Mordecai seems out of place in the middle of the description of Esther's preparations, but gives evidence against her having been delivered at once to Ahasuerus, as stated in 2:8. (See n. 2:8–16, above.)

2:14 Shaashgaz appears to be a junior eunuch, answerable to Hegai.

2:15 Esther's relationship with Mordecai has already been explained in 2:7, as has her parentage, and there is no clear need for her to be identified again. What the new information adds is the apparent name of her father, Abihail (*Avichayil*), but since this is a translation of 'my father of valour', it may have been more a daughter's description than a name. Since 'my father of valour' could not have been used by Mordecai, it is given here as an E text, together with the note about Mordecai that follows. (NB: *chayl*, a variant of *chayil*, means 'army' and appears in 1:3 in *chayil parus oomaduy* (the army of Persia and Media).

2:15 'Everyone who saw Esther adored her.' This is one of numerous sentences that sit awkwardly in the narrative, interrupt it and give the appearance of having been added later.

2:16 The dating of Esther's initiation contains the first reference to a specific month: until now, the only time marker has been to the 180-day party held in the third year of Ahasuerus's reign. There is no need to attribute monthly dating to E except that to do otherwise breaks M's narrative flow (unless it can be said that mensual measure is gendered). The reference is interesting, however, by virtue of its duality. The month is announced first by its ordinal position in the calendar (the tenth month) as it would have been known to the Jewish population—which had not previously had names for all the months and seems only to have adopted Akkadian names when exiled to Babylon—and only afterwards by name (Tevet). This gives strong evidence for the Book of Esther's having been written at a time when Tevet was still a new usage that needed explanation. See also 3:7 (Niysan), 3:13 (Adar), 8:9 (Siyvan), 8:12 (Adar), and 9:1 (Adar). References subsequent to 9:1 are exclusively to the name of the month and not its ordinal position.

2:18 There is no evidence here to suggest that Esther's coronation was either immediate or even in Tevet, as some commentators have suggested.

2:19 'And the virgins were gathered again …' seems to be an incomplete fragment.

2:20 'And Mordecai sat in the king's gate …' seems to be an incomplete fragment.

2:19–20: See above. The coupling of two incomplete fragments is one of several examples of bilateralism that has been taken as linear.

2:20 See n.2:10.

2:21 The first we learn about Mordecai is that he walks daily to the court of the king's harem (2:11). We now learn that it was his custom to sit in the king's gate, which is presumably the entrance to the king's private quarters rather than the entrance to the stronghold of Shushan. By tradition, city gates were where the elders of a community would sit, but it is also where beggars gathered and where tax officials were positioned, to extract levies on imports. What the status was of Mordecai or any others who sat in the gateway to the king's compound cannot be known, except that 3:2–3 suggests that it was packed with the king's guards and other retinue.

2:21 The guards Bigthan and Teresh are referred to as eunuchs, as is Hathach in verse 4:5. (See n.2:3.)

2:21 Bigthan appears as Bigthana in the E text at 6:2.

Chapter Three

3:1 No reason is given for Haman's sudden rise to power.

3:4 If it is disadvantagous to be Jewish in the Persian court, or more widely (as Mordecai's warning to Esther suggests), it is not clear why Mordecai now excuses his refusal to bow to Haman by declaring his Jewish identity. It cannot be that the rise of Haman has made the position of Jews less precarious, and Mordecai has already sworn Esther to secrecy about her background. With Haman's elevation, their being Jewish makes them more vulnerable.

3:7 Oddly, the casting of lots was carried out, presumably by Haman's friends, before Haman had yet proposed his idea of genocide to the king. The description of this is dense and unclear: the text explains what the first month was, in which year of the king's reign the casting of lots took place, and what the word *pur* meant, but not how the casting worked. A loose translation has therefore been ventured to try to make sense of it.

3:7 The word *pur* was unknown in Hebrew until the Book of Esther. The usual word for 'lot' was *goral*. In Leviticus 16:8 et seq., Aaron is told to cast *goralot* over two goats. In the Book of Jonah, the sailors cast *goralot* to identify who had caused the storm at sea. During the *Kol Nidrei* service on *Yom Kippur*, the congregation sings to God (in *Ki anu amechah*) 'we are God's inheritance and you are *goraleinu*' (our lot or destiny). The Hebrew *pur* is an adaptation of an Akkadian word (*pūru*) used by the Baylonians, and this further reinforces the Book of Esther's neo-Babylonian character. See also 9:24 and 9:26.

3:7 Regarding the identifying of the month, see n.2:16.

3:10 The repetition (see 3:1) of 'the son of Hammedatha the Agagite' here (and in 8:5, 9:7, 9:24) suggests that 'the son of Hammedatha the Agagite' was a formal title.

3:12 This verse is the first to focus on a particular day: 13 Niysan (formerly Aviv). The new name of the month was given in 3:7.

3:12 The recipients of Haman's command are identified twice: first in terms of (a) the local officials installed by the king to govern his provinces and (b) the people's own rulers; and then in terms of (c) the official languages of the provinces and (d) the local languages as actually spoken. The difference in tone of the two listings contains built-in assumptions that make one or other list redundant. They are therefore assigned to M and E.

3:13 Regarding the identifying of the month, see n.2:16.

3:13–15 The publication of Haman's decree is

described here in three different formulas. Verse 13 and verse 15 both start by saying that the decree was sent by messengers on horseback (i.e. posts). Verse 13 and 14 talk about the decree being published in every province. Apart from these two duplications, verse 13 identifies the victims and the planned date of the massacre. Verse 14 makes clear that the edict is meant to incite the masses and give them time—eleven months—to prepare their attack. Verse 15 adds that the stronghold of Shushan was not exempted, which is significant in the light of the suggestion at the end of the verse that those who lived at the heart of the empire, in the city of Shushan, were not entirely happy with what was being ordered.

Chapter Four

4:1 The Hebrew *saq* gives us the English word 'sack' or 'sackcloth'.

4:2 For the note about not being able to enter the king's gate dressed in sackcloth, see the Introduction.

4:3 et seq. There is a brief split in the narrative at this point. The first two lines of Chapter Four have concentrated on Mordecai in Shushan; in 4:4 Mordecai's reaction to Haman's decree is reported to Esther by her maidens and chamberlains, and she responds to the embarrassment of discovering that her step-father is wearing inappropriate clothes outside the king's apartments by sending him clean clothes, which he refuses. Esther here apparently knows nothing about the decree or the weeping in the provinces, only that her step-father is behaving oddly. Verse 4:3, stuck between 4:2 and 4:4 introduces a different theme. We now learn that all the Jews of the provinces are in turmoil. Esther (having, we must assume, heard about this) asks a servant to go to Mordecai to find out why. From the character of the writing, the rest of this chapter ought to be all E text. It is Hathach, Esther's servant, who acts as go-between, tells Esther what Mordecai has learnt about the forthcoming massacre and hands over Mordecai's written evidence, and everything follows from that. It is not Hathach, however, who reports back to Mordecai Esther's unwillingness to intercede but an unidentified 'they': *vayagidu l'Mordechai et-divrei Esther* ('and *they* told Mordecai Esther's

words'). The only 'they' already referred to in this chapter is the maidservants and chamberlains in the M text at 4:4. Had Hathach been reporting back to Mordecai, the Hebrew would have said *yag'ed* in the singular. This requires us to ascribe the text from 4:12 onwards to M; we might even ascribe 4:7–8 to M on the grounds that Mordecai is only talking about himself and Shushan, not about the provinces which is what she asked about in the E text at 4:5. If we do so, however, we cannot explain how Esther has found out about the proclamation or Mordecai's plea that she intercede. For clarity, therefore, we need to return to a consolidated text at 4:6, which deals with information known to both an M and an E narrator, even if the style of the writing from this point argues against our doing so. (The chapter would be a lot easier if 4:3 appeared after 4:4; then the two texts could be treated as linear and sequential, with Esther's inquiry about the distress in the provinces following her response to news of Modercai's personal torment.)

4:6–11 In this account, there is no mention of Mordecai's unusual appearance, as there is in the M text; by contrast, Hathach finds Mordecai in the town square as usual and all seems normal. Whether Mordecai knows what is happening in the provinces is not clear. He does however know about the proclamation posted in Shushan and the threat to the Jews living in the citadel. He gives a full account of this to Hathach, provides written evidence and begs him to beg Esther to beg the king to intervene. She does not regard Mordecai's report as sufficiently urgent, however; she is more concerned with the insecurity of her own position. She fears that the king has not called for her for a month and that her novelty to him may have worn off, and she is aware that to ask for a royal favour without being first invited is punishable by death. So untroubled is she by the condition of her people that she does not even tell Mordecai that she cannot comply with his request: he has to learn this from others.

4:13–14 The first turning point in the *Megillah* occurs when Mordecai spells out to Esther that her present vulnerability is as nothing compared to what is likely to happen at the end of the year, suggesting that her marriage into royalty is perhaps part of the divine plan. His urging comes with a threat, however: if Esther does not act now and someone else does, she will be regarded by that saviour not as part of the Jewish community but as an enemy or traitor, and treated accordingly, i.e., she faces death whatever she does. Given her earlier reluctance, it can be asked whether her change of behaviour follows a change of heart: whether she is now acting primarily in the interests of her people or only of herself; whether she has been radicalised by Mordecai; and whether she is now on a journey —from childhood to adulthood, innocence to understanding, and passivity to leadership. Her initial motives are unclear.

4:15 Only now does Esther accept that her life is forfeit anyway and that she needs to take steps to save her people in order to save herself. From here on, it is Esther who takes over the initiative from Mordecai, who steps back to let the machinery of the court gear up. Having received news that Esther at last has a plan, Mordecai goes off and 'does everything that Esther has commanded him' (4:17). This reversal of roles eventually, however, leads to a power struggle—gendered and generational—between the two of them, and this is reflected in the text's non-linearity.

4:16 It is not clear from the text whom the three-day fast called by Esther is meant to appease. God is not mentioned. The implication seems to be that it is Ahasuerus who is being appealed to, assuming that the fasting is brought to his attention.

Chapter Five

5:1–3 The fifth chapter also begins with what looks like E text, and with events that could only have been known to an E narrator. To ascribe these lines to E, however, removes the narrative bridge linking the end of Chapter Four to the M text at 5:4—the next point of divergence—and must therefore be presented as consolidated text.

5:4–14 There are two responses to the king's question at 5:3, asking what Esther wants. In the M text, at 5:4, Esther asks that the king and Haman immediately attend a banquet—in fact, a drinking party or symposium, in the Greek sense—that she has hastily prepared and where she hopes to put her petition more formally. The king agrees, insists that Haman also hurry to attend, and there asks Esther again what she

wants. Her answer is not given until two chapters later, at 7:3–4, where she at last identifies herself as Jewish by telling the king of the threat to her life and to the life of her people. Typically of M, this is a plain, straightforward narrative. By contrast, in the alternative E text, at 5:8, Esther answers the king's question by asking him and Haman to attend a banquet the next day. The delay allows time for two interruptions, both to Haman's considerable disadvantage. The first (5:9–14) tells how Haman returns to his wife and friends, puffed up with pride at the honours that now seem to be racing his way, and of his delight at their suggestion that he ask the king to hang Mordecai so that he can better enjoy Esther's drinking party; the second (6:4–14) deals with the follow-up to the Bigthan and Teresh story and the sudden and overdue catapaulting of Mordecai to prominence. The two pairs of stories—Haman's rise and fall and Mordecai's eclipsing—are the most satisfying moments in the *Megillah*. Told with drama and pathos, and buffed by the irony of Haman's self-preening, they offer the reader the sweetest pleasure: a ringside seat at the defeat of the smug. The E text at 7:2 then brings Esther to the same point of petitioning that was left hanging in the M text at the end of 5:6. In short, each text now refers to two inquiries by the king, one banquet invitation from Esther, and one banquet. This is more plausible than the standard linear text which asks us to accept three inquiries by the king, two invitations and two banquets, all of which recalls the arguably spurious duplication of the king's parties in the first chapter. Duplication is, admittedly, a feature of ancient formal rhetoric, as Esther's speech illustrates, e.g., at 5:7—'my petition and my request' (*sh'eilatiy u'vakashatiy*)—and in her appeal to the king at 8:5–6, but triplication is certainly not.

5:4 and 5:8 Esther's choice of a drinking party rather than a banquet is not so much indicative of her awareness of the king's liking for drink as of the use of wine to formalise and celebrate policy decisions. At 3:15, the king and Haman sit down and drink to confirm their decision to eradicate Jewry from the empire.

5:5 Both the M text here and the E text at 6:10 and 6:14 make a point of the king's hurrying Haman. The implication in all three cases is that Haman is being hurried against his will and otherwise would not exert himself to satisfy the queen's wishes, and this is the first sign of a potential fracture between him and the king. The E text also contrasts this entertainingly with Haman's hurrying home in humiliation (at 6:12).

5:6 For commentary on *v'yinatein* ('[and] it shall be granted'), see n.7:2.

Chapter Six

6:1–14 The whole of this chapter, plus the next two lines, looks like E text. It consists of a night-time interlude, the equivalent of a Shakespearean aside, in which a chance element—the king's sleeplessness—triggers a decisive change of plot direction. Here, the psychology of the king is played off against that of Haman, who badly misreads him. What at 6:6 is clear to the reader, but not to Haman, who has little self-awareness, is that in asking what should be done to the man whom the king delights to honour, Ahasuerus is setting Haman up, but it is unclear why. Mordecai has gone unrewarded after saving the king's life and the king—waking up to a truth, rather as the prophet Jonah does *en route* to Tarshish, that a wrong needs putting right—blames Haman; without further textual evidence, however, the subsequent disgracing of Haman seems immense and arbitrary to us. In terms of where the story is heading, it is also premature: the king does not know that Haman has come to ask for Mordecai to be hanged, nor has Esther yet denounced Haman or unveiled Mordecai as her relative and protector. Ahasuerus has therefore not yet had any obvious reason to question his decision to endorse Haman's planned genocide of his empire's Jews. We can only speculate, therefore, on whether readers might once have been able to read into the text some other tension—structural or personal— between the Persian king and his aristocratic Babylonian prime minister (see Introduction) or whether arbitrariness—the same arbitrariness that sees Ahasuerus at a stroke countermand his decree against the Jews—was simply regarded as the privilege of kingship.

6:2 Bigthana. See n.2:1.

Chapter Seven

7:2 The king's E-text inquiry at the end of this line functions in the same way as his M-text inquiry at the end of 5:6. Both invite the crucial plea that Esther makes at 7:3, and both are almost identically worded—'Whatever thy petition it shall be granted thee and whatever thy request even to the half of the kingdom it shall be performed'. There are however two differences in the second version: the interpolation of 'Queen Esther' after 'Whatever thy petition' (*mah sh'eilateich*) and the substitution of a feminine verb (*v'tinatein*) for a masculine (*v'yinatein*) in the second 'and it shall be granted'. A feminine verb '*v'teiat*' (and it shall be performed) also follows 'whatever thy request' (*mah bakashateich*). The reason for the feminisation of the verb is unclear. In every previous reference to Esther's request (one in 5:3 and two in 5:6), what is being given is not directly the kingdom (or half the kingdom)—*chatsiy hamalchoot*—which is feminine but the abstraction *mah bakashateich* and *mah sh'eilateich* ('whatever your request' and 'whatever your petition'), and abstractions are by convention masculine. The noun and the verb only correspond, therefore, in 5:3 and in the first case in 5:6, where both are masculine. In the second example in 5:6 and here in 7:2, the verbs are both feminine. Later, in 9:12, *mah sh'eilateich* correctly takes a masculine verb (*v'yinatein*) and *mah bakashateich* wrongly takes a feminine verb (*v'teiat*). It is no solution to say that the verb is responding not to the noun but to what is being referred to—half the kingdom— because then all the masculine verbs are wrong. There are other unexplained gender incongruities in the Bible (*Tanach*) but there seems to be no systematic study of them. The Turkish-born Safed kabbalist Rabbi Moshe Alshich (1508–1593) has suggested that the masculine verb in 5:3 is a reference to Ahasuerus's giving Esther a gift because he is stronger than her, but appears in its feminine form in 7:2 because she is now as strong as him and deserves what she asks for by right, but this only illustrates that commentators have no adequate explanation.

7:3 At the point where Esther finally makes her plea, the text reverts to the consolidated format.

7:4 Esther brilliantly calibrates her plea to

Ahasuerus. She makes clear that what she is asking for is that the king guarantee her life and that of her people, rather than merely the conditions of their existence. 'If we were merely to be sold into captivity, I would not have bothered you' is a clever bargaining ploy.

7:9 Re: Harvonah, see n.1:10.

Chapter Eight

8:1 According to this line, it was not until Chapter Seven that Esther finally revealed her relationship with Mordecai.

8:4–6 These three lines seem like an alternative to Esther's simpler and self-sufficient M-text request in 8:3. What 8:4–6 does is to re-state her plea, adding the details of how what she said was worded. As noted in the Introduction, her wording contains two sets of internal duplications, one in line 5, the other in line 6. It is not clear whether these duplications are intentionally poetic and rhetorical, in the style of the Psalms, or whether they are themselves duplications or alternative versions retained by the redactor[s]. The novelty introduced at the end of line 5 is that the king's annulment should be published in writing, as the original decree had been, for the avoidance of doubt. Ahasuerus agrees to this in 8:8.

8:9 The record of who should receive copies of the annulment is split into an M text and E text, each of which lists two different or alternative groups of recipients: M places the Jews first; E places them second. As in 3:12, the E text notes that the king's words were translated into the languages of the various provincial recipients.

8:9 Regarding the identification of the month, see n.2:16.

8:10, 8:14 The mode of delivery of the king's edict is duplicated in an M text and an E text.

8:11, 8:13 In addition to the annulment of Haman's decree, the king has now added that the Jews may avenge themselves on their enemies, and the details of this are more extensive in the M text than the E text. Whether the inspiration for this revenge attack is the king's or Esther's or

Mordecai's is ambiguous; that it might be theirs rather than his is implied by his invitation in 8:8: 'Write ye also as it pleaseth you'. The plural here (*v'atem kitvoo* ...) shows that the invitation was issued to them jointly.

8:12 The M text adds a date for the revenge attack: 13th Adar. Regarding the identification of the month, see n.2:16.

8:15–16 When the *Megillah* is read at Purim, these lines are spoken (more often shouted) first by the entire congregation and then repeated by the leader. See also 2:5 and 10:3.

8:17 Either this line anticipates the celebrations referred to in Chapter Nine or these are other, preliminary, spontaneous celebrations held in the response to the news of the king's new decree.

8:17 'And many from among the peoples of the land became Jews.' Rabbinic Judaism does not hugely welcome converts but this line—which, if the *Megillah* is a comedy, must be one of the most comic—suggests a greater fluidity in pre-rabbinic times. Whether contemporary Judaism would have accepted the prospective converts' motives—self-preservation rather than religious belief—is a real theological question.

8:17 For 'for the fear of the Jews was fallen upon them,' see n.9.2–3.

Chapter Nine

9:1 The two last phrases in 9:1 interrupt the flow of the main sentence, and seem like editorial additions. They function here not as alternates but as call-and-response, the E text giving added nuance to the more declarative M text.

9:1 Regarding the identification of the month, see n.2:16.

9:2–3: These two lines continue the antiphonal call-and-response structure initiated at the end of 8:17. In each case, the phrases or sentences are terminated or interrupted by a phrase about the people's fear. The lines are different, however. At 8:17, where 'the peoples of the land' has just been invoked, the response is 'for the fear of the Jews was fallen upon them.' At 9:2, where the reference is to 'no man' [literally: 'a man could not …'], the response is 'for the fear of the Jews was fallen upon all the peoples.' These are both given here as E texts. Line 9:3, which is about the king's civil service, is given as an M text, not least because what had been fear of the Jews now attaches to Mordecai ('for the fear of Mordecai had fallen upon them').

9:4   Following the reference to Mordecai in 9:3, two explanations are given for why he now commands fear: again, each is significantly nuanced. The M text speaks of Mordecai in terms of a senior figure at the heart of the king's court: a man with a growing imperial reputation; the E text treats him more like a member of the family ('the man Mordecai'): someone one knows too well to be awed by, who happens to be enjoying a lucky break.

9:5 et seq. Difficulties with who did what when start in earnest at 9:5. The king has decreed that the Jews may slaughter their enemies, but on one day only: 13th Adar, the twelfth month. In the standard linear text, unspecified numbers ('all their enemies') are killed in the provinces on that day and 500 are killed in Shushan fortress including Haman's ten sons. At 9:11, the king marvels at what has happened in Shushan and at what may have happened elsewhere in his empire and, apparently tantalised by the killings, tempts Esther to request permission for further bloodshed, which she readily does. She then asks that Haman's sons be killed again, which makes no sense unless she simply wants the bodies hung out for all to see, which is not the obvious reading of the text. (The Hebrew would have explained the purpose if the hanging was not the execution that it seems to be. See Introduction, fn.6.) There follows a sequence of passages that repeat similar phrases but that fit together illogically, interrupt the line or lines of thought, and defy chronology. This incoherence is troubling but can be resolved by unravelling the text into separate threads; indeed, it can only be so resolved.

a) The two conflicting references to Haman's sons need to be apportioned one each to M and E. Thus, according to M, Haman's sons are among those killed on 13 Adar (9:7–10) and it is thus only in the M text that the king refers to their killings (at 9:12). By contrast, the sons are not killed in the E account until Esther specifically asks for this to happen (9:13) and for it to be carried out by royal decree. The significant difference is that in the first case, the sons are killed by the Jews, albeit by permission of the king, whereas in the second case they are executed by the state. That is, what Esther has done is to get the king to acknowledge that Haman has committed a heinous crime against the state for which the sons' killing is elevated to state-sanctioned capital punishment and for which—should there ever be any doubt—the Jews are guiltless.

b) Ascribing to M Esther's plea that the Jews be granted a second day of killing (9:13) solves the problem of achronicity because it limits all reference to the second day of killings to M. Now, E says nothing about a second day; instead Esther asks for the sons to be hanged and then the E text answers the king's question about what might have happened in the provinces. In the linear text, this reads as a rhetorical question ('if the Jews have killed 500 in Shushan fortress plus the ten sons of Haman, what on earth have they done in the rest of my empire?'). Separating the text in 9:12 changes the king's remark from an exclamation of amazement into a simple request for information, which is answered at 9:16: the Jews killed 75,000.

c) Separating the text in this way solves the linear problem of referring to events of 14th Adar before referring to the events in the provinces of 13th Adar. Now, the M text goes on to talk about 14th Adar, following Esther's M text request for an additional day, while the E text merely continues to elaborate what happened on 13th Adar. This is followed immediately, and logically, by the E text note that the provincial Jews carried out their killings on 13th Adar and celebrated on the day after.

d) This sequence—from 9:5 to 9:19—is rounded off by a pair of balancing summaries. M records that the Jews of Shushan killed on 13th and 14th Adar and celebrated on 15th; the E text records that the rural Jews of the provinces did all their killing on 13th Adar and celebrated on 14th Adar.

e) Apportioning the texts associates Mordecai with events inside Shushan fortress and the queen with events in the provinces. Mordecai seems to be interested in affairs of state, Esther with the interests and liberties of her people as a whole.

9:15–16 The repeated phrase 'but on the spoil they laid not their hand' (*oovabizah lo shalchoo et-yadam*) recalls a primary concept of virtue in the Bible. Abraham (*Avram*) in Genesis 14:23 tells the king of Sodom that he has sworn to God 'I will not take a thread nor a shoe-latchet nor aught that is thine, lest thou shouldest say: I have made Abram rich.'

9:17–19 The ends of each sentence introduce another call-and-response chorus: 9:17: 'they rested on the fourteenth day of the same and made it a day of feasting and joy; 9:18: 'they rested on the fifteenth day of the same and made it a day of feasting and joy; 9:19: '[they] make the fourteenth day of the month Adar a day of joy and feasting'. See also n.9:19.

9:19 The E text records that in future years, rural Jews got into the habit of celebrating Purim as a one-day festival on 14 Adar. The M text at 9:23 disagrees. See n.9:20 et seq.

9:20–24 A second division reveals a growing split between Esther and Mordecai. In this five-line M-text passage, Mordecai is seen trying to unify the Jewish people by proposing (9:21) that all Jews celebrate their victory not just on 14th Adar but on 15th Adar. He wants Jews in the provinces and Jews in Shushan to celebrate their own festival and each other's. That they have agreed to do so, and that it was Mordecai who persuaded them, is insisted on by the M text at 9:23. As noted above (n.9:19), however, this is at odds with the E text. The contradiction is best represented as two texts in conflict. Making 9:20–24 follow 9:19 as a single linear text makes no sense.

9:24 The meaning of *pur* has already been explained in 3:7. There seems no obvious reason for the text to repeat it.

9:25 Since the M text has just tried to bring the story of Purim to an end by giving all credit to Mordecai and ignoring Esther, the E text now summarises events by crediting Esther and ignoring Mordecai. In each case, the texts place the stress differently. Mordecai is most concerned that Purim be remembered by a two-day festival that he has ordained; Esther mainly wants her agency respected.

9:26–28 Since the E text has just ignored Mordecai's insistence on a two-day festival, the M text reiterates it.

9:29–32 The E text here takes over and presents a coda that ascribes all responsibility for the Jews' victory to Esther. The simple E text now identifies her in terms of her birth parentage ('daughter of Abihail'), stresses that it was she who wrote letters to the 127 provinces and deployed all her authority in doing so, notes that the provincial Jews had decided to keep Purim in their own way ('spoke peace and truth … as they had ordained for themselves and for their seed') and grants their independent decision her royal support. This is a radical challenge to Mordecai and one that the M text tries to sabotage. It insists on Mordecai's equality as Esther's parent ('daughter of Abihail *and of Mordecai*') and adds a line to suggest that what Esther was in fact writing to confirm was his second letter insisting on a two-day festival. In the face of Esther's challenge, the M text then repeats (at 9:30) that it was he and not she who wrote to the Jews in the provinces, and co-opts Esther's name to reinforce his claim. This is, in short, a fight for supremacy between Esther and Mordecai and one that the linear text does its best to disguise.

Chapter Ten

10:1–3 This brief closing chapter is entirely M text and gives Mordecai the last word. No mention is made of Esther. It is Mordecai's greatness that is praised; Esther, the eponymous hero of the book, is sidelined. The reason can only be guessed at.

Appendix: The Septuagint Megillah

Addition A
Mordecai's Dream (Prologue)

1 In the second year of the reign of Ahasuerus the great, on the first day of the month of Niysan, Mordecai, the son of Jair, the son of Shimei, the son of Kish, of the tribe of Benjamin, had a dream. 2 He was a Jew, and dwelt in the city of Susa, a great man, who was a servant in the king's court. 3 He was also one of the captives whom Nebuchadnezzar, king of Babylon, had exiled from Jerusalem with Jeconiah, king of Judea; 4 and this was his dream: Behold a noise of a tumult, with thunder and earthquakes and uproar in the land: 5 And behold, two great dragons came forth ready to fight, and their cry was great. 6 And at their cry all nations were prepared to battle, that they might fight against the righteous people. 7 And lo, a day of darkness and gloom! Affliction and anguish! Oppression and great chaos upon the earth! 8 And the whole righteous nation was troubled, fearing their own evils, and were ready to perish. 9 Then they cried unto God, and upon their cry, as if from a little fountain, arose the greatest flood and many overflowing waters. 10 The light and the sun rose up, and the lowly were exalted, and devoured those held in esteem. 11 Now when Mordecai, who had seen this dream, and what God had determined to do, was awake, he kept this dream in mind, and until night by all means desired to understand it.

12 And Mordecai took his rest in the court with Gabatha and Tharra, the two eunuchs of the king, and keepers of the palace. 13 And he heard their plan, and searched out their purposes, and learned that they were about to lay hands upon Ahasuerus the king; and so he testified to the king about them. 14 Then the king interrogated the two eunuchs, and after they had confessed, they were strangled. 15 And the king made a record of these things, and Mordecai also wrote thereof. 16 So the king commanded Mordecai to serve in the court, and for this he rewarded him. 17 However, Haman, the son of Hammedatha the Agagite, was highly esteemed by the king and sought to injure Mordecai and his people because of the king's two eunuchs.

Chapter One

1 Now it happened after these matters in the days of Ahasuerus (this is Artaxerxes who reigned from India even to Ethiopia, over one hundred and twenty-seven provinces), 2 that in those days, when the King Ahasuerus sat on the throne of his kingdom, whose palace was in Susa, 3 in the third year of his reign, he made a feast for all his princes and his servants; and the power of Persia and Media, the nobles and princes of the provinces, were before him. 4 And after these things, after he had displayed the riches of his glorious kingdom and the honour of his excellent majesty for many days, even one hundred and eighty days, 5 when the days of the wedding feast were fulfilled,[1] the king made a seven-day wine party for all the people who were present in Susa, the palatial city, both great and small, in the court of the garden of the king's palace. 6 There were hangings of fine linen and flax

---

1 The Greek text is explicit about the king's banquet being a celebration of his wedding (to Vashti): ὅτε δὲ ἀνεπληρώθησαν αἱ ἡμέραι τοῦ γάμου.

on cords of fine linen and purple, fastened to golden and silver studs, on pillars of Parian marble and stone. The couches were of gold and silver, on a pavement of emerald stone, and of pearl, and of Parian stone, and open-worked coverings variously flowered, with roses worked round about. 7 They gave them drinks in gold and silver vessels, and a small cup of carbuncle set out of the value of thirty thousand talents, and royal wine in abundance, which the king himself drank. 8 In accordance with the law, the drinking was not compulsory; for so the king had instructed all the officials of his house, that they should do according to every man's wishes.

9 And Vashti [Astin/Oastin] the queen made a feast for the women in the royal house which belonged to King Ahasuerus.

10 On the seventh day, when the heart of the king was merry with wine, he commanded Mehuman, Biztha, Harbona, Bigtha, and Abagtha, Zethar, and Carcass,[2] the seven eunuchs who served in the presence of Ahasuerus the king, 11 to bring Vashti the queen before the king with the royal crown, to show the people and the princes her beauty; for she was beautiful. 12 But Queen Vashti/Astin refused to come at the king's commandment by the eunuchs. Therefore the king was very angry, and his anger burned in him. 13 Then the king said to his friends,[3] 'What shall we do to the queen Vashti/Astin according to law, because she has not done the bidding of the King Ahasuerus by the eunuchs?' 14 So Arkesaeus, and Sarsathaeus, and Malesear, the princes of the Persians and Medes, who were near the king, who sat chief in rank by the king, drew near to him, 15 and reported to him according to the laws how it was proper to do to queen Vashti/Astin, because she had not done the things commanded of the king by the chamberlains.[4] 16 And Memucan[5] answered before the king and the princes, 'Vashti/Astin the queen has not done wrong to just the king, but also to all the princes, and to all the people who are in all the provinces of the King Ahasuerus. 17 For this deed of the queen will become known to all women, causing them to show contempt for their husbands, when it is reported that King Ahasuerus commanded the queen to be brought in before him, but she did not come.' 18 Today, the princesses of Persia and Media who have heard of the queen's deed will tell all the king's princes. This will cause much contempt and wrath. 19 If it please the king, let a royal commandment go from him, and let it be written among the laws of the Medes and the Persians, so that it cannot be altered, that Vashti may never again come before King Ahasuerus; and let the king give her royal estate to another who is better than she. 20 When the king's decree, which he shall make, is published throughout all his kingdom (for it is great), all the wives will give their husbands honour, both great and small.' 21 This advice pleased the king and the princes, and the king did according to the word of Memucan:[6] 22 for he sent letters into all the king's provinces, into every province according to its writing, and to every people in their language, that every man should rule his own house, speaking in the language of his own people.

Chapter Two

1 After these things, when the wrath of King Ahasuerus was pacified, he no longer mentioned[7] Vashti/Astin, remembering what she had said and how he had condemned her. 2 Then the king's servants who served him said, 'Let beautiful young virgins be sought for the king. 3 Let the king appoint officers in all the provinces of his kingdom, that they may gather together beautiful young virgins to Susa, the palatial city, to the harem, to the custody of [Hegai,] the king's eunuch, keeper of the women. Let cosmetics and other care be given them; 4 and let the maiden who pleases the king be queen instead of Vashti.' The idea pleased the king, and he did so.

5 Now there was a certain Jew in Susa, the palatial city, whose name was Mordecai, the son of Jair,

2 In other translations: 'Aman [or Haman] and Bazan and Thara and Barazi [or Boraze] and Zatholtha and Abataza and Tharaba.'

3 In other translations: 'The king said to his wise men, who knew the times, (for it was the king's custom to consult those who knew law and judgment; and the next to him were Carshena, Shethar, Admatha, Tarshish, Meres, Marsena, and Memucan, the seven princes of Persia and Media, who saw the king's face, and sat first in the kingdom) . . .'.

4 Verses 14 and 15 are absent in other translations.

5 In other translations: 'Muchaeus' or 'Mouchaios'.

6 Or 'Muchaeus'. See n.A4.

7 The Greek verb ἐμνήσθη means 'remembered' but some English versions render this as 'mentioned' to avoid the contradiction of not remembering and remembering. The same problem recurs elsewhere in the Bible, notably with the blotting out of the memory of Amalek but also remembering immemorially the evil that he did (see Exodus 17:14 and Deuteronomy 25:17–19).

the son of Shimei, the son of Kish, a Benjamite,[8] 6 who had been carried away from Jerusalem with the captives who had been carried away with Jeconiah king of Judah, whom Nebuchadnezzar the king of Babylon had carried away. 7 He brought up Hadassah, that is, Esther, his uncle's daughter;[9] for she had neither father nor mother. The maiden was fair and beautiful; and when her father and mother were dead, Mordecai took her for his own daughter. 8 So it happened, when the king's commandment and his decree was heard, and when many maidens were gathered together to Susa, the palatial city, to the custody of Hegai,[10] that Esther was taken into the king's house, to the custody of Hegai, keeper of the women. 9 The maiden pleased him, and she obtained kindness from him. He quickly gave her cosmetics and her portions of food, and the seven choice maidens who were to be given her out of the king's house. He moved her and her maidens to the best place in the harem. 10 And Esther had not revealed who her people or her relatives were, because Mordecai had instructed her that she should not make it known. 11 And every day, Mordecai walked in front of the court of the women's quarters, to find out how Esther was doing, and what would become of her.

12 Each young woman's turn came to go in to King Ahasuerus after her purification for twelve months (for so were the days of their purification accomplished, six months being rubbed with oil of myrrh and six months with sweet fragrances and with preparations for beautifying women). 13 Then she would go in to the king: and whatever she desired was given her to go with her out of harem to the king's house. 14 In the evening she would go in, and on the next day would return into the second harem, to the custody of Shaashgaz,[11] the king's eunuch, who kept the concubines. She went in to the king no more, unless the king delighted in her and she was called by name.

15 Now when it was time for Esther, the daughter of Abihail/Aminadab, the uncle of Mordecai, who had taken her for his daughter, came to go in to the king, she required nothing but what [Hegai] the king's eunuch, the keeper of the women, advised. For Esther obtained favour in the sight of all those who looked at her. 16 So Esther was taken to King Ahasuerus, into his royal house, in the tenth month, which is the month of Tevet,[12] in the seventh year of his reign. 16 And the king loved Esther more than all the women, and she obtained favour and kindness in his sight more than all the virgins; so that he set the royal crown on her head, and made her queen instead of Vashti.[13] 18 Then the king made a great feast for all his princes and his servants, even Esther's feast; and he proclaimed a holiday in the provinces, and gave gifts according to the king's bounty.[14]

19 Now Mardochaeus was serving in the palace. 20 And Esther had not revealed who her kindred were; for so Mordecai had commanded her, to fear God, and perform his commandments, as when she was with him: and Esther did not behave differently now she was no longer living with him. 21 And two of the king's chamberlains/eunuchs, [Bigtha and Teresh,] the chiefs of the bodyguard, were grieved, because Mordecai had been promoted; and they sought to kill King Artaxerxes. 22 And the matter was told to Mordecai, and he made it known to Esther, and she declared to the king the matter of the conspiracy. 23 And the king interrogated the two chamberlains, and had them hanged from a tree: and the king gave orders to make a note for a memorial in the royal records [the *Book of the Chronicles*] of the good offices of Mordecai, as a commendation.[15]

8 The classic translation of the Septuagint Book of Esther (1851) by Sir Lancelot Charles Lee Brenton has: 'Mardochaeus, the [son] of Jairus, [the son] of Semeias, [the son] of Cissaeus'.

9 In other translations: 'And he had a foster child, daughter of Aminadab, his father's brother' ('Αμιναδὰβ ἀδελφοῦ πατρὸς αὐτοῦ).

10 In other translations: 'Gai'.

11 In other translations: 'Gai'.

12 In other translations: 'in the twelfth month, which is Adar' (τῷ δωδεκάτῳ μηνί, ὅς ἐστιν 'Αδάρ).

13 In other translations: 'he put on her the queen's crown' or 'he set the queen's diadem on her' with no mention of Vashti.

14 In other translations: 'and set free those whom he had imprisoned'.

15 This version contains no mention of God or of piety; Esther is merely loyal to Mordecai. In other translations, it is her loyalty to God that is emphasised: 'Now Esther had not identified her kindred; for so Mardochaeus commanded her, to fear God, and perform his commandments, as when she was with him: and Esther changed not her manner of life' (ἡ δὲ 'Εσθὴρ οὐχ ὑπέδειξε τὴν πατρίδα αὐτῆς· οὕτως **γὰρ ἐνετείλατο αὐτῇ Μαρδοχαῖος, φοβεῖσθαι τὸν Θεὸν** καὶ ποιεῖν τὰ προστάγματα αὐτοῦ, καθὼς ἦν μετ' αὐτοῦ καὶ 'Εσθὴρ οὐ μετήλλαξε τὴν ἀγωγὴν αὐτῆς).

Chapter Three

1 After these things King Ahasuerus promoted Haman the son of Hammedatha the Agagite,[16] and advanced him, and set his seat above all the princes who were with him. 2 All the king's servants who were inside the king's gate bowed down, and paid homage to Haman; for the king had so commanded concerning him. But Mordecai did not bow down or pay him homage. 3 Then the king's servants, who were inside the king's gate, said to Mordecai, 'Why do you disobey the king's commandment?' 4 Now it came to pass, when they spoke daily to him, and he did not listen to them, that they told Haman, to see whether Mordecai's reason would stand; for he had told them that he was a Jew. 5 When Haman saw that Mordecai did not bow down, nor pay him homage, Haman was full of wrath. 6 But he scorned the thought of laying hands on Mordecai alone, for they had made known to him Mordecai's people. Therefore Haman sought to destroy all the Jews, the people of Mordecai, throughout the whole kingdom of Ahasuerus.[17] 7 In the first month, which is the month of Niysan, in the twelfth year of King Ahasuerus, they cast *Pur*, that is, the lot, before Haman from day to day, and from month to month, and chose the twelfth month, which is the month of Adar. 8 And so Haman said to King Ahasuerus, 'There is a certain people scattered abroad and dispersed among the peoples in all the provinces of your kingdom, and their laws are different from those of other peoples. They do not keep the king's laws. Therefore it is not to the king's benefit to allow them to remain. 9 If it please the king, let it be written that they be destroyed; and I will pay ten thousand talents of silver into the hands of those who are in charge of the king's business, to bring it into the king's treasuries.'[18] 10 The king took his ring from his hand, and gave it to Haman the son of Hammedatha the Agagite, the Jews' enemy, to seal the decree. 11 The king said to Haman, 'The silver is yours; the people also. Do with them what you will.' 12 Then the king's scribes were called in on the first month, on the thirteenth day of the month; and all that Haman commanded was written to the king's satraps, and to the governors who were over every province, from India even to Ethiopia, to one hundred and twenty-seven provinces and to the rulers of every people, to every province according its writing, and to every people in their language. 13 It was written in the name of King Ahasuerus, and it was sealed with the king's ring. Letters were sent by couriers into all the king's provinces, to destroy, to kill and to cause to perish, all Jews, both young and old, little children and women, in one day, on the thirteenth day of the twelfth month,[19] which is the month of Adar, and to plunder their possessions.

Addition B
The Royal Decree

13a This is a copy of the letters: 'The great king Ahasuerus writes these things to the princes and governors who are under him from India unto Ethiopia in one hundred and twenty-seven provinces. 13b "After I became lord over many nations and had dominion over the whole world, not lifted up with presumption of my authority, but carrying myself always with equity and mildness, I purposed to settle my subjects continually in a quiet life, and make my kingdom peaceable and open for passage to the utmost coasts, to renew peace, which is desired of all men. 13c But when I asked my counselors how this might be brought to pass, Haman, who excels in wisdom among us and was approved for his constant good will and steadfast fidelity and had the honour of the second place in the kingdom, 13d declared to us that in all nations throughout the world there was scattered a certain malicious people, who had laws contrary to all nations and continually despised the commandments of kings, so that the uniting of our kingdoms, honourably intended by us, cannot go forward. 13e Seeing this, we understand that this people alone is continually in opposition unto all men, differing in the strange ways of their laws and bringing about evil to our state, working all the mischief they can, so that our kingdom may not be firmly established. 13f Therefore have we commanded that all those who are signified in writing to you by Haman, who is ordained over these affairs and is

---

16 In other translations; 'Aman [son] of Amadathes, the Bugaean'.

17 In other translations, line 6 is much shorter: 'He took counsel to destroy utterly all the Jews who were under the rule of Artaxerxes.'

18 In other translations, merely: 'and I will remit into the king's treasury ten thousand talents of silver.'

19 Other translations have the killing marked for first day of the month, or to take place in one day. 'One day' seems more accurate: ἐν ἡμέρᾳ μιᾷ μηνὸς δωδεκάτου'.

next unto us, shall all, with their wives and children, be utterly destroyed by the sword of their enemies, without all mercy and pity, by the fourteenth day of the twelfth month of Adar of this present year. 13g Thus may they, who from of old and now also are malicious, may in one day with violence go into the grave, and so ever hereafter cause our affairs to be well settled and without trouble.'

Chapter Three (continued)

14 Copies of the letter were published in every province, that the people should be ready against that day. 15 The couriers went forth in haste by the king's commandment, and the decree was given out in Susa. Then the king and Haman sat down to drink; but the city of Susa was troubled.

Chapter Four

1 Now when Mordecai found out all that was done, Mordecai tore his clothes and put on sackcloth with ashes and went out into the midst of the city and wailed loudly and bitterly [that a nation that has done no wrong is going to be destroyed].[20] 2 He came even before the king's gate, for no one is allowed inside the king's gate clothed in sackcloth.

3 In every province, wherever the king's commandment and his decree came, there was great mourning among the Jews with fasting and weeping and wailing; and many lay in sackcloth and ashes.

4 Esther's maidens and her eunuchs came and told her this, and the queen was exceedingly grieved. She sent clothing to Mordecai, to replace his sackcloth; but he did not accept it. 5 Then Esther called for Hathach,[21] one of the king's eunuchs, whom he had appointed to attend her, and commanded him to go to Mordecai, to find out what this was and why it was. 6 So Hathach went out to Mordecai, to the city square which was before the king's gate.[22] 7 Mordecai told him of all that had happened to him and the exact sum of the money that Haman had promised to pay to the king's treasuries for the destruction of the Jews. 8 He also gave him the copy of the writing of the decree that was given out in Susa to destroy them, to show it to Esther,

and to declare it to her, and to urge her to go in to the king, to make supplication to him and to make request before him, for her people.

9 Hathach came and told Esther all these words.[23] 10 Then Esther spoke to Hathach, and gave him this message for Mordecai: 11 'All the king's servants and the people of the king's provinces know that whoever, whether man or woman, comes to the king into the inner court without being called, there is one law for him, that he be put to death, except those to whom the king might hold out the golden sceptre that he may live. I have not been called to come in to the king these thirty days.' 12 They[24] told Esther's words to Mordecai. 13 Then Mordecai asked them to return answer to Esther: 'Do not think to yourself that you will escape in the king's house any more than all the Jews. 14 For if you remain silent now, then relief and deliverance will come to the Jews from another place, but you and your father's house will perish. Who knows if you have not come to the kingdom for such a time as this?' 15 Then Esther asked them to answer Mordecai: 16 'Go, gather together all the Jews who are present in Susa and fast for me: neither eat nor drink three days, night or day. I and my maidens will also fast the same way. Then I will go in to the king, which is against the law; and if I perish, I perish.' 17 So Mordecai went his way and did according to all that Esther had commanded him.

Addition C: Prayers of Mordecai and Esther

17a Then Mordecai thought upon all the works of the Lord and made his prayer unto him, saying, 17b 'O Lord, Lord, the King Almighty, the whole world is in your power and if you have appointed to save Israel, then no man can contradict you: 17c For you have made heaven and earth and all the wondrous things under the heavens. You are Lord of all things; there is no man who can withstand you, for you are the Lord. 17d You know all things and you know, Lord, that it was neither in

23 In some translations, v.9 is made up of a longer passage: 'Hathach came and told Esther the words of Mordecai: "Remember," he said, "the days of your humiliation, when I nurtured you in my hand, because Haman, who is second only to the king, is against us to the death. And you, invoke the Lord and persuade the king for us and free us from death."'

24 Or 'Hathach' or 'Achrathaeus', etc.

20 The passage in square brackets does not appear in all translations.
21 In other translation: 'Achrathaeus' or 'Hachrathaios'.
22 This verse is missing in some translations.

contempt nor pride nor for any desire of glory that I did not bow down to proud Haman. For I would have been content, with good will for the salvation of Israel, to kiss the soles of his feet. 17e But I did not, so that I might not prefer the glory of man above the glory of God: neither will I worship any but thee, O God; neither will I do so in pride. 17f And now, O Lord God and King, God of Abraham, spare thy people, for their eyes are upon us to bring us to naught; yes, they desire to destroy the inheritance which has been yours from the beginning. 17g Despise not the people whom you delivered out of Egypt for your own self. 17h Hear my prayer and be merciful to your inheritance: turn our sorrow into joy, so that we may live, O Lord, and praise thy name; and destroy not the mouths of those who praise thee, O Lord.'

17i And all Israel, in the same way, cried out most earnestly to the Lord, because their death was before their eyes.

17j Queen Esther also was in fear of death and resorted to the Lord. And she put away her glorious apparel, and put on the garments of anguish and mourning; and instead of precious ointments, she covered her head with ashes and dung; and she humbled her body greatly, and all the aspects of her beauty she covered with her torn hair. And she prayed to the Lord God of Israel, saying, 17k 'O my Lord, you alone are our King. Help me, a desolate woman, who has no helper but you, for my danger is close at hand. 17l From my youth I have heard, in the tribe of my family, how you, O Lord, took Israel from among all peoples, and our fathers from all their predecessors, for a perpetual inheritance, and you have performed whatsoever you promised them. 17m And now we have sinned before you; therefore you have given us into the hands of our enemies, because we worshiped their gods. O Lord, you are righteous! 17n Nevertheless, it does not satisfy them that we are in bitter captivity, but they have struck a deal with their idols. They will abolish the purpose that you with your mouth have ordained, and destroy your inheritance, and silence the mouth of those who praise you, and quench the glory of your house and of your altar, 17o and open the mouths of the heathen to bring forth the praises of the idols, to magnify a fleshly king for ever. 17p O Lord, do not give your sceptre to those who are nothing, and let them not laugh at our fall; but turn their schemes upon themselves, and make an example of him who began this against us. 17q Remember, O Lord, make yourself known in the time of our affliction and give me boldness, O King of the nations and Lord of all power. 17r Give me eloquent speech in my mouth before the king; turn his heart to hate him that fights against us, so that there may be an end of him and of all that are likeminded to him. 17s But deliver us with your hand and help me, for I am desolate and have no other help but you. 17t 'You know all things, O Lord; you know that I hate the glory of the unrighteous and abhor the bed of the uncircumcised and of all the heathen. 17u You know my necessity, for I abhor the sign of my high estate, which is upon my head in the days when I show myself, and that I abhor it as a menstrual rag, and that I wear it not when I am in private by myself. 17v You know that your handmaid has not eaten at Haman's table, and that I have not greatly esteemed the king's feast, nor drunk the wine of the drink offerings. 17w Neither has your handmaid had any joy, since the day that I was brought here to the present, except in you, O Lord God of Abraham. 17x O mighty God above all, hear the voice of the forlorn and deliver us out of the hands of the mischievous and deliver me out of my fear.'

Addition D:
Esther Before the King

1a On the third day, when she ended her prayers, she put away her mourning garments and put on her glorious apparel. 1b And being gloriously adorned, after she called upon God, who knows all and saves all, she took two maids with her; and on the one, she leaned, carrying herself daintily, and the other followed, bearing up her train. 1c She was blooming in the perfection of her beauty, and her countenance was cheerful and very amiable, but her heart was in anguish out of fear. 1d Then, having passed through all the doors, she stood before the king, who sat upon his royal throne and was clothed with all his robes of majesty, all glittering with gold and precious stones; and he was very dreadful. 1e Then, lifting up his countenance which shined with majesty, he looked very fiercely upon her; and the queen collapsed and went pale and fainted and her head drooped upon the head of the maid who went before her. 1f Then God changed the spirit of the king into mildness, and in fear he leaped from his throne and took her in his arms, till she came to again, and he comforted her with loving words and said to her, 1g 'Esther, what is the matter? I am your brother, be of good cheer. You shall not die, though our commandment be general. Come near.' 1h And so he held up his golden sceptre, and laid it upon her neck, and embraced her, and said, 'Speak to me.' 1i Then she said to him, 'I saw you, my lord, as an angel of God, and my heart was troubled for fear of your majesty. For you are wonderful, lord, and your countenance is full of grace.' 1j And as she was speaking, she fainted [again] and fell. Then the king was troubled and all his servants comforted her.

Chapter Five

1 Then the king asked her, 'What would you like, Queen Esther? What is your request? It shall be given you even to half of the kingdom.' 2 Esther replied, 'Today is my lucky day. If it seems good to the king, let the king and Haman come today to the banquet[25] that I will prepare for him.' 3 Then the king said, 'Bring Haman quickly, so that it may be done as Esther has said.' So the king and Haman came to the banquet[26] that Esther had prepared. 4 The king said to Esther at the banquet of wine,[27] 'What is your petition? It shall be granted you. What is your request? Even to half of the kingdom it shall be performed.' 5 Then Esther answered and said, 'My petition and my request is this. 6 If I have found favour in the sight of the king, and if it please the king to grant my petition and to perform my request, let the king and Haman come to the banquet that I will prepare for them, and I will do the same.' 7 Then Haman went out that day joyful and glad of heart. But when Haman saw Mordecai in the king's gate, that he did not stand up or move for him, he was filled with wrath against Mordecai. 8 Nevertheless Haman restrained himself and went home. There he sent and called for his friends and Zeresh his wife. 9 Haman recounted to them the glory of his riches, the multitude of his children, all the things in which the king had promoted him, and how he had advanced him above the princes and servants of the king. 10 Haman also said, 'Yes, Esther the

25 τὴν δοχήν.
26 τὴν δοχήν.
27 ἐν δὲ τῷ πότῳ.

Queen allowed no man to come in with the king to the banquet that she had prepared but myself; and tomorrow I am also invited by her together with the king. 11 Yet all this avails me nothing, as long as I see Mordecai the Jew sitting at the king's gate.' 12 Then Zeresh his wife and all his friends said to him, 'Let a gallows be made fifty cubits high, and in the morning speak to the king about hanging Mordecai on it. Then go in merrily with the king to the banquet.' This pleased Haman, so he had the gallows made.

Chapter Six

1 That night, the king could not sleep. He commanded his servant to bring him the book of records of the chronicles, and they were read to the king. 2 It was found written that Mordecai had told of [Bigtha and Teresh,] two of the king's eunuchs, who were doorkeepers, who had tried to lay hands on the King Ahasuerus. 3 The king said, 'What honour and dignity has been bestowed on Mordecai for this?' Then the king's servants who attended him said, 'Nothing has been done for him.' 4 The king said, 'Who is in the court?' Now Haman had come into the outer court of the king's house, to speak to the king about hanging Mordecai on the gallows that he had prepared for him. 5 The king's servants said to him, 'Behold, Haman stands in the court.' The king said, 'Let him come in.' 6 The king said to him, 'What shall be done to the man whom the king delights to honour?' Now Haman said in his heart, 'Who would the king delight to honour more than myself?' 7 Haman said to the king, 'For the man whom the king delights to honour, 8 let royal clothing be brought which the king uses to wear, and the horse which the king rides on, and the royal crown which is set upon his head. 9 Let the clothing and the horse be delivered to the hand of one of the king's most noble princes, that they may array the man whom the king delights to honour with them, and have him ride on horseback through the city square, and proclaim before him, 'Thus shall it be done to the man whom the king delights to honour!' 10 Then the king said to Haman, 'Hurry and take the clothing and the horse, as you have said, and do this for Mordecai the Jew, who sits at the king's gate. Let nothing fail of all that you have spoken.' 11 Then Haman took the clothing and the horse, and arrayed Mordecai, and had him ride through the city square, and pro-

claimed before him, 'Thus shall it be done to the man whom the king delights to honour!' 12 [After that,] Mordecai came back to the king's gate, but Haman hurried home, mourning and his head hidden under his cloak. 13 Haman recounted to Zeresh his wife and all his friends everything that had happened to him. Then his wise men and Zeresh his wife said to him, 'If Mordecai, before whom you have begun to fall, is of Jewish descent, you will not prevail against him, but you will surely fall before him, for the living God is with him.' 14 While they were talking, the king's eunuchs came to hurry Haman to the banquet that Esther had prepared.

Chapter Seven

1 So the king and Haman went to drink with [Esther,] the queen. 2 The king said again to Esther, on the second day at the banquet of wine, 'What is your petition, Queen Esther? It shall be granted you. What is your request? Even to half of the kingdom it shall be performed.' 3 Then Esther the queen answered, 'If I have found favour in your sight, O king, and if it please the king, let my life be granted me at my petition, and my people at my request. 4 For both I and my people are sold for destruction, for pillage and for slavery, we and our children for bondmen and bondwomen, and I have said nothing, for the slanderer is not worthy of being at the king's court.'[28] 5 Then King Ahasuerus said to Esther the queen, 'Who is he and where is he, who dared presume in his heart to do so?' 6 Esther said, 'An adversary and an enemy, even this wicked Haman!' Then Haman was afraid before the king and the queen. 7 The king stood up in his wrath from the banquet of wine and went into the palace garden. Haman rose to make request for his life to Esther the queen; for he saw that he was in a difficult position. 8 When the king returned out of the palace garden, Haman was prostrate on the couch where Esther was, begging her mercy. Then the king said, 'Will he even assault the queen in front of me in the house?' As the word went out of the king's mouth, Haman's face fell. 9 Then Harbona,[29] one of the eunuchs who were with the king said, 'Behold, Haman has made a gallows fifty cubits high for Mordecai, who spoke good for the king, and it is standing ready at Haman's house.' The king said, 'Hang him on it!' 10 So they hanged Haman on the gallows that he had prepared for Mordecai. Then the king's wrath was pacified.

Chapter Eight

1 On that day, King Ahasuerus gave the house of Haman, the Jews' enemy, to Esther the queen. Mordecai was called to the king; for Esther had revealed how he was related to her. 2 The king took off his ring, which he had taken from Haman, and gave it to Mordecai. And Esther set Mordecai over all that had been Haman's. 3 Now Esther spoke again before the king, and fell down at his feet and begged him with tears to put away the mischief of Haman the Agagite, and his plan that he had devised against the Jews. 4 Then the king held out to Esther the golden sceptre. So Esther arose and stood before the king. 5 She said, 'If it pleases the king and if I have found favour in his sight, and if it seems right to the king and I am pleasing in his eyes, let it be written to reverse the letters devised by Haman, the son of Hammedatha the Agagite, which he wrote to destroy the Jews who are in all the king's provinces. 6 For how can I endure to see the evil that would come to my people? How can I endure to see the destruction of my kindred?' 7 Then King Ahasuerus said to Esther and to Mordecai the Jew, 'See, I have given you the house of Haman, and have hanged him on the gallows, because he laid his hand on the Jews. 8 Write also to the Jews, as it pleases you, in the king's name, and seal it with the king's ring; for the writing which is written in the king's name and sealed with the king's ring may not be reversed by any man.' 9 So the king's scribes were called at that time, in the third month, which is Siyvan,[30] on the twenty-third day of the month; and it was written according to all that Mordecai commanded to the Jews, and to the satraps, and the governors and princes of the provinces which are from India to Ethiopia, one hundred and twenty-seven provinces, to every province according to its writing, and to every people in their language, and to the Jews in their writing, and in their language. 10 And the letters were written in the name of King Ahasuerus, and sealed with his ring, and sent by couriers [on horseback,

28 In other translations, Esther says that she has spoken out, but possibly in the sense of her soul having rebelled within her.

29 In other translations: 'Bugathan'.

30 In other translations: 'in the first month, being Niysan'.

riding on royal horses that were bred from swift steeds].[31] 11 In those letters, the king granted the Jews who were in every city to gather themselves together, [to defend their life, to destroy, to kill and] to cause to perish all [the power of the people and province][32] that would assault them, [their little ones and women, and to plunder their possessions,][33] 12 on one day in all the provinces of King Ahasuerus, on the thirteenth day of the twelfth month, which is the month of Adar:

Addition E
The Counter–Decree

12a And the following is the copy of the letter of the orders. 12b 'The great king Ahasuerus sends his greetngs to the princes and governors of the one hundred and twenty-seven provinces from India to Ethiopia and to all our faithful subjects. 12c Many who have been frequently honoured with the great bounty of their gracious princes have conceived ambitious designs, and not only endeavour to hurt our subjects, but moreover, not being able to bear prosperity, they also endeavour to plot against their own benefactors 12d And they hope not only to abolish gratitude from among men, but also, elated by the boastings of men who are strangers to all that is good, imagine they shall escape the sin-hating vengeance of the ever-seeing God. 12e Oftentimes, also, the pleasing words of those who are trusted to manage their friends' affairs, have caused many in authority to be complicit in taking innocent blood and have enwrapped them in remediless calamities—thus beguiling the innocence and goodness of princes with the falsehood and deceit of their lewd disposition. 12f Now you may see this, as we have declared, not so much by reading ancient histories but by looking at what has been wickedly done of late, through the pestilential behaviour of those unworthily placed in authority. 12g We must take care, in future, that our kingdom may be quiet and peaceable for everyone, 12h both by adopting [necessary] changes and by always judging things which come before us with truly equitable proceedings. 12i For Haman, a Macedonian, the son of Hammedatha, being an alien, not of Persian blood, and disagreeing

markedly with our mild form of government, but having been hospitably entertained by us, 12j had obtained so much of the favour that we show to every nation, that he was called our father and was continually honoured above all as the person next to the king. 12k But he, not bearing his great dignity, went about to deprive us of our kingdom and life, 12l and, by manifold and cunning deceits, sought of us the destruction also of Mordecai, who saved our life and continually procured our good, as also of blameless Esther, partaker of our kingdom, with their whole nation. 12m For by these means he thought, finding us destitute of friends, to have transferred the kingdom of the Persians to the Macedonians. 12n But we find that the Jews, whom this wicked wretch had consigned to utter destruction, are no evildoers, but live by most just laws, 12o and that they be children of the most high and most mighty living God, who has ordered the kingdom both unto us and unto our progenitors, in the most excellent way. 12p Wherefore, you shall do well not to obey the letters sent to you by Haman the son of Hammedatha, for he, who was the worker of these things, is hanged at the gates of Susa with all his family: God, who rules all things, speedily rendering vengeance to him according to his deserts. 12q Therefore you shall publish the copy of this letter in all places that the Jews may freely live after their own laws. And you shall aid them, so that even on the same day, the thirteenth day of the twelfth month of Adar, they may be avenged on them, who in the time of their affliction would have set upon them. 12r For Almighty God has turned to joy for them the day wherein the chosen people would have perished. 12s You shall therefore keep it as a high day among your solemn feasts, with all feasting: that both now and hereafter there may be safety for us and the well-meaning Persians; but for those who conspire against us, a memorial of destruction. 12t Therefore every city and country whatsoever which does not do according to these things shall be destroyed without mercy with fire and sword and shall be made not only unacceptable for men, but also most hateful to wild beasts and fowl for ever.'

Chapter Eight (continued)

13 So let the copies be posted conspicuously throughout the kingdom, and let all the Jews be ready against this day, to fight against their ene-

---

31 This passage is absent from other translations.
32 This passage is absent from other translations.
33 This passage is absent from other translations.

mies. 14 So the couriers who rode on royal horses went out, hastened and pressed on by the king's commandment. The decree was given out in Susa, the palatial city. 15 And Mordecai went out from the presence of the king in royal clothing of blue and white, and with a great crown of gold, and with a robe of fine linen and purple; and the city of Susa shouted and was glad. 16 The Jews had light, gladness, joy and honour. 17 In every city and province, wherever the decree was published, wherever the proclamation was announced, there was joy and gladness among the Jews, and many of the Gentiles were circumcised and became Jews; for the fear of the Jews had fallen upon them.

Chapter Nine

1 In the twelfth month, which is the month Adar, on the thirteenth day, the time came for the king's commandment to be put into execution, 2 on that day, the adversaries of the Jews perished: for no one resisted, through fear of them. 3 For the chiefs of the satraps, and the princes and the royal scribes, honoured the Jews, for the fear of Mardochaeus lay upon them. 4 And the order of the king was in force, that he should be celebrated in all the kingdom.[34] 5 And the Jews slew [and] smote all those who hated them [with the] stroke of the sword and slaughter and destruction and did just as they thought appropriate to those who hated them. 6 In Susa, the palatial city, the Jews killed and destroyed five hundred men. 7 They killed Parshandatha, Dalphon, Aspatha, 8 Poratha, Adalia, Aridatha, 9 Parmashta, Arisai, Aridai, and Vaizatha,[35] 10 the ten sons of Haman the son of Hammeda-

tha, the Jews' slanderer, but they did not lay hands on the plunder.[36] 11 On that day, the number of those who were slain in Susa, the palatial city, was brought to the king. 12 The king said to Esther, 'The Jews have slain and destroyed five hundred men in Susa, the palatial city, including the ten sons of Haman; what then have they done in the rest of the king's provinces! And what is your petition? It shall be granted you. What is your further request? It shall be done.' 13 Then Esther said, 'If it pleases the king, let it be granted to the Jews who are in Susa to do tomorrow also according to this day's decree, and let Haman's ten sons be hanged on the gallows.' 14 The king permitted it to be so done; and he gave to the Jews of the city the bodies of the sons of Aman to hang. 15 The Jews who were in Susa gathered themselves together on the fourteenth day of the month of Adar, and killed three hundred men in Susa; but they did not lay their hand on the spoil.

16 The other Jews who were in the king's provinces gathered themselves together, defended their lives, had rest from their enemies, and killed seventy-five thousand[37] of those who hated them; but they did not lay their hand on the plunder. This was done on the thirteenth day of the month of Adar; 17 and on the fourteenth day of that month they rested and kept it as a day of feasting and gladness. 18 But the Jews in Susa assembled again on the fourteenth days of the same month; and they rested on the fifteenth day of that month, and made it a day of feasting and gladness. 19 That is why those Jews who are dispersed in villages, and who live in unwalled towns, make the fourteenth day of Adar a day of gladness and feasting, a good day, and a day of sending presents of food to one another.

20 Mordecai wrote these things in a book and sent letters to all the Jews who were in all the provinces of the king Ahasuerus, both near and far, 21 to enjoin them that they should keep the fourteenth and fifteenth days of the month of Adar yearly as joyful days, 22 as the days in which the Jews had rest from their enemies, and the month which was turned for them from sorrow to gladness and from mourning into a good day; that they should make them days of feasting and gladness and of sending presents of food to

34 In other translations, a longer version of verses 2 to 4 appears: 'on the day when the enemies of the Jews had hoped to conquer the (but it was turned out the opposite happened, that the Jews conquered those who hated them), the Jews gathered themselves together in their cities throughout all the provinces of the King Ahasuerus, to lay hands on those who wanted to harm them. No one could withstand them, because the fear of them had fallen on all the people. All the princes of the provinces, the satraps, the governors, and those who did the king's business, helped the Jews, because the fear of Mordecai had fallen on them. For Mordecai was great in the king's house and his fame went out throughout all the provinces; for the man Mordecai grew greater and greater.

35 Other translations name Haman's sons as: 'Pharsannes, Delphon, Phasga, Pharadatha, Barea, Sarbaca, Marmasima, Ruphaeus, Arsaeus and Zabuthaeus'.

36 Other translations suggest that there was plundering.

37 In other translations: 'fifteen-thousand'.

one another and gifts to the needy. 23 The Jews accepted the custom which they had begun, as Mordecai had written to them, 24 because Haman the son of Hammedatha, the Agagite, the enemy of all the Jews, had plotted against the Jews to destroy them and had cast '*pur*,' that is the 'lot', to consume them and to destroy them; 25 and how he had told this to the king, and how the king had commanded by letters that Haman's wicked plan, which he had devised against the Jews, should return on his own head, and that he and his sons should be hanged on the gallows. 26 Therefore they called these days 'Purim,'[38] from the word '*pur*', because of all the words of this letter and of what they had seen concerning this matter and of what had come to them. 27 And they established it, and imposed it on themselves and on their descendants and on all those who joined themselves to them, so that it should not fail, that they would keep these two days according to what was written and according to its appointed time every year; and that these days should be remembered and kept throughout every generation, every family, every province, and every city; 28 and that these days of Purim should not fall from among the Jews, nor their memory perish from their seed.

29 Then Esther the queen, the daughter of Abihail/Aminadab, and Mordecai the Jew, wrote with all authority to confirm this second letter of Purim. 30 And Mordecai and Esther the queen appointed [a fast] for themselves privately, even at that time also having formed their plan against their own health. 31 And Esther established it by a command for ever, and it was written for a memorial.

Chapter Ten

1 King Ahasuerus laid a tribute on the land and on the islands of the sea. 2 All the acts of his power and of his might, and the full account of the greatness of Mordecai, to which the king promoted him, behold, they are written in the *Book of the Chronicles of the Kings of Media and Persia*. 3 And Mordecai the Jew took over from King Ahasuerus, and was great among the Jews, and accepted by the multitude of his brothers, seeking the good of his people and speaking peace to all his descendants.

Addition F
Interpretation of the Dream (Epilogue)

3a Then Mordecai said, 'God it is who has done these things. 3b For I remember a dream which I saw that concerned such matters, and nothing thereof has failed. 3c A little fountain became a river, and there was light and the sun and much water: this river is Esther, whom the king married and made queen; 3d and the two dragons are myself and Haman. 3e And the nations were those which were assembled to destroy the name of the Jews; 3f and my nation is this Israel, which cried to God and was saved, for the Lord has saved his people, and the Lord has delivered us from all those evils, and God has wrought signs and great wonders, which have not been done among the Gentiles. 3g Therefore he has made two lots, one for the people of God and another for all the Gentiles. 3h And these two lots came at the hour and time and day of judgment, before God among all nations. 3i So God remembered his people and justified his inheritance. 3j Therefore those days shall be given to them in the month of Adar, the fourteenth and fifteenth day of the same month, with an assembly and joy and with gladness before God, according to the generations for ever among his people.'

3k In the fourth year of the reign of Ptolemeus and Cleopatra, Dositheus, who said he was a priest and Levite, and Ptolemy his son, brought this letter of Purim, which they said was the same, and Lysimachus the son of Ptolemeus, who was in Jerusalem, translated it.

The End

---

38 In other translations: 'Phrurae'.

More non-fiction from EnvelopeBooks

Lost Levant | Rupert de Borchgrave
In 2003 Rupert de Borchgrave set off on a journey of ideas that took him to the much-disputed grounds where the ancient world constructed the philosophical, religious, mathematical and artistic thinking that went on to shape our culture. This book is the product of that journey and the musing that it gave rise to.

A Road to Extinction | Jonathan Lawley
When Britain took over the Andaman Islands in 1857, the welfare and independence of its African pygmy inhabitants was of no concern. Nine tribes died out. Dr Lawley now assesses survival prospects for the three remaining tribes and weighs up the legacy of his grandfather, who ran the colony in the early 1900s.

Artist Spy Prisoner | George Tomaziu
Artist George Tomaziu was imprisoned and tortured in 1944 by Romania's fascist government for monitoring Nazi troop movements through Bucharest during the Second World War but imagined that his heroism would be recognised if Romania ever became free. He was terribly mistaken. Three years after the war ended he was imprisoned again, now by Romania's Communists, this time for thirteen years.

Postmark Africa | Michael Holman
Made an 'Amnesty Prisoner of Conscience' while under house arrest as a student in Rhodesia, Michael Holman went on to document Africa's emergence from colonialism as Africa Editor of the *Financial Times*. This book is a must-read introduction to Africa's dreams of independence and their subsequent demise.

Why My Wife Had To Die | Brian Verity
There is no known cure for Huntington's disease, a wasting condition that its victims acquire from a parent. In this painful account, the author vents his rage at society, lawmakers, health services and the Church for not grasping the need, as he sees it, to legalise compulsory sterilisation and assisted dying.

The West and the Rest | Ian Ross
Having worked in the oil and tobacco industries, Ian Ross argues that trade is objectively more creative than democracy in bridging cultural divisions. Where diplomats are necessarily restrained by caution, principle and public accountability, business executives are incentivised to be forward-looking, adaptable, unprejudiced and trusting. A personal story and an eye-opener.

Wembley Speaks: A Year in the Life of a London Suburb | Stephen Games
How do people talk to each other, react to each other, give and ask for advice, conciliate, commiserate and laugh? In a modern reconstruction of Mayhew's landmark 19th-century social study, EnvelopeBooks turns to the Nextdoor social networking app to observe a community engaging with itself on day-to-day issues. A priceless archive.

How to Rescue a Tiger: And Other Animals | Roger Allen

Multi-award-winning news photographer Roger Allen documents the dramatic animal rescue missions he has brought to world attention – of tigers, lions, rhinos, dogs and bears – as well as, in many cases, their happy outcomes, in a vivid series of true-life stories, that illustrate the dark side of our love of animals.

From Bedales to the Boche | Robert Best

Bedales, the progressive boarding school founded by J.H. Badley in 1893, instilled values that sustained many of its pupils for the rest of their lives. Robert Best recalls its influence on him as an enthusiastic army recruit in 1914 and, from 1916, in the Royal Flying Corps which, against the odds, he survived.

A Question of Paternity | David Tereshchuk

TV reporter David Tereshchuk has traveled the world questioning the perpetrators of injustice and their victims, but could never prise one answer from his own mother: who his father was. Her evasion set him off on a life of insecurity and alcoholism. And a quest.

The Martyrdom of Ahmad Shawkat | Michael Goldfarb

When Gulf War II broke out in 2003, Ahmad Shawkat became guide and translator to NPR-reporter Michael Goldfarb. After the fall of Saddam, Ahmad set up a cultural magazine, published eleven issues and was assassinated for publicly decrying Islamic terror. This is his story. A *TLS* Book of the Year.

Flights of Fancy: The Love Letters of Margaret McLaren-Reid | Richard Cullen

During the sunset of British imperialism, Margaret McLaren-Reid and her ace-pilot husband lived an elite existence marked by privilege but also isolation, stationed in the Middle East, India and South America. Richard Cullen reconstructs the sense of unease that service families endured, based on 740 handwritten letters dating from the early 1920s that lift the veneer of order and prestige.

Fiction from EnvelopeBooks

The Very Annoying Jew | Michael Kretzmer

Burnt-out TV executive David Britton has had enough of the business he has made a career in, not just because of its ideological sloganising and immaturity but because of its cruelty. His collision with his own company comes to a head when he tries to protect a vulnerable member of staff from being forced into gender reassignment surgery to boost ratings on a podcast for non-binary viewers. Powerful satire.

The Green Man | Dan Jones

After humiliating a fellow inquisitor at a trumped-up witch trial in Northern Italy, Brother Jacobus of Vienna is intrigued by rumours of strange events in Northern England. In defiance of the cardinals in Avignon, he travels to Berwick where he finds a land in disarray, beset by Scottish raiders, eccentric Franciscan friars and talk of demons in the woods. Can he explain this pagan revival and keep his faith and reason intact?

Mrs Woodbine's Prejudices | Michael Ladner

Prof. Arthur Lash, born Artur Lasch in pre-war Austria, takes his American wife and their three sons back to Vienna, in 1960, to see how well his father is rebuilding a life interrupted by Germany's annexation of Austria in 1938. For Arthur, the journey helps re-establish his links with the city he grew up in; for the rest of his family, other emotions are awoken, all watched over by their disregarded but loyal family nanny.

A Sin of Omission | Marguerite Poland

An emotionally intense novel, set in 1870s South Africa at a time of rising anti-colonial resistance. The book examines the tragedy of a promising black preacher, hand-picked for training in England as a missionary, then neglected by the Church he loves. Winner, 2021 *Sunday Times* CNA 'Book of the Year' Award.

Printed in Great Britain
by Amazon

67790eef-c9e7-46fc-ae28-a555542c9032R02